UNDERSTANDING
FEEDBACK

A critical exploration for
eacher educators

Critical Guides for
Teacher Educators

You might also like the following titles from Critical Publishing.

Becoming a Teacher Education Researcher
Ed Diane Mayer and Ian Menter
ISBN: 9781913453299

Tackling Anxiety in Primary Mathematics Teachers
By Karen Wicks
ISBN: 9781913453015

The Teacher Educator's Handbook: A narrative approach to professional learning
By Elizabeth White
ISBN: 9781913453657

Using Digital Video in Initial Teacher Education
By John McCullagh
ISBN: 9781913453336

Our titles are also available in a range of electronic formats. To order, or for details of our bulk discounts, please go to our website www.criticalpublishing.com or contact our distributor NBN International by telephoning 01752 202301 or emailing orders@nbninternational.com.

UNDERSTANDING
FEEDBACK

A critical exploration for
teacher educators

Series Editor: Ian Menter

Caroline Elbra-Ramsay

First published in 2021 by Critical Publishing Ltd

British Library Cataloguing in Publication Data
A CIP record for this book is available from the British Library

ISBN: 9781913453251

This book is also available in the following e-book formats:
MOBI: 9781913453268
EPUB: 9781913453275
Adobe e-book reader: 9781913453282

Cover and text design by Greensplash Limited

Project Management by Deanta Global Publishing Services, Dublin, Ireland

Typeset by Deanta Global Publishing Services, Chennai, India

Critical Publishing

3 Connaught Road

St Albans

AL3 5RX

www.criticalpublishing.com

Paper from responsible sources

CONTENTS

ACKNOWLEDGEMENT

This book is based on my PhD thesis entitled *Navigating the Pedagogical, Relational and Moral Economies of Assessment: An Analysis of the Development of Student Teachers' Understandings of Feedback.*

DEDICATION

I would like to thank the wonderful student teachers who participated in the study on which this book is based. They were generous with their time throughout, and their engagement and enthusiasm for the project was personally inspiring and motivating. Interviewing each of them was a genuine privilege. It was an experience that gave me total faith in the next generation of reflective and thoughtful teachers. I wish them every success in their careers.

I would also like to thank friends, family and colleagues who supported me in both my original PhD study and the writing of this text.

Lastly, as the text has been finalised during Lockdown 3 of the Covid pandemic, I would like to acknowledge the hard work, perseverance and resilience of the entire teaching community, whose commitment to the profession, in the most challenging of circumstances, has been incredible.

ABOUT THE SERIES EDITOR

Ian Menter is former President of BERA, 2013–2015. At Oxford University Department of Education, he was Director of Professional Programmes and led the development of the Oxford Education Deanery. Before moving to Oxford, Ian was Professor of Teacher Education at the University of Glasgow. Prior to that he held posts at the University of the West of Scotland (Dean of Education and Media), London Metropolitan University (Head of School of Education), University of the West of England and the University of Gloucestershire. Ian was President of the Scottish Educational Research Association from 2005 to 2007 and chaired the Research and Development Committee of the Universities' Council for the Education of Teachers from 2008 to 2011. He is a Fellow of the Academy of Social Sciences and a Fellow of the Royal Society of Arts and is a Visiting Professor at Bath Spa University and Ulster University and an Honorary Professor at the University of Exeter. Since 2018 he has been a Senior Research Associate at Kazan Federal University, Russia.

ABOUT THE **AUTHOR**

Caroline Elbra-Ramsay is the Deputy Head of the School of Education, Language and Psychology at York St John University, working largely in initial teacher education provision. Prior to this, Caroline was a primary school teacher for 16 years, teaching across Key Stages One and Two and the Foundation Stage. This included a deputy headship of a large primary school where Caroline had responsibility for school assessment. This began a longstanding interest in assessment and, more specifically, feedback. As an initial teacher educator, Caroline teaches primary English, philosophy for children and professional studies, which includes working with student teachers to develop their own assessment and feedback practice in school. Her own research has also focused on assessment and feedback, most recently in her PhD, from which this text is drawn.

FOREWORD

It is paradoxical that feedback is such a core element in educational processes that it is frequently taken for granted. This can be the case even within the processes of initial teacher education, where, as Caroline Elbra-Ramsay points out very early in this book, it has at least a dual aspect. Beginning teachers will certainly be learning how to provide feedback to the pupils they are working with in classrooms, but at the same time they will also themselves be receiving feedback from the more experienced professionals with whom they are working, whether those are teachers or higher education tutors. What Caroline offers in this volume is one of the most careful analyses of feedback processes in teacher education that has been published.

Drawing on her own doctoral study, she explores the complex nature of feedback and locates it within the discourses of assessment as well as within the regulatory frameworks within which teacher education takes place. She relates her discussion most directly to the teaching standards that exist in the context of England, but the relevance of her insights extends far beyond to the rest of the UK and indeed internationally. I am confident that this book will be of enormous interest to teacher educators – and their students – all over the world.

What is particularly effective here is Caroline's skill in combining very thorough scholarship with a sense of the practical demands and challenges faced by teacher educators in their daily work. This is exactly what the books in this series seek to do, that is, to provide research-based support to colleagues who are undertaking one of the most important roles in contemporary society, preparing teachers to work with the citizens of the future.

In defining feedback through three distinctive 'economies' – the pedagogical, the relational and the moral – she provides us with a highly original and focused set of insights that will influence how we understand the processes of feedback that are so critical in the complex learning processes that occur within teacher education.

Ian Menter
Series Editor, Critical Guides for Teacher Educators
Emeritus Professor of Teacher Education, University of Oxford

This chapter explores the following critical issues:

- why this book is necessary;

- whether there is a disconnect between the potential of feedback and how it is experienced and understood;

- the rapid development of initial teacher education (ITE) in England;

- the extent to which teacher education includes both learning and teaching and the influences on this distinction;

- how both learning and teaching will therefore influence how student teachers understand feedback.

Why this book?

In the twenty-first century we are surrounded by feedback. We are bombarded with messages requesting feedback about our purchases, experiences and interactions and repeatedly assured that others 'take your feedback seriously'. Every organisation seems interested in what we, as consumers in the widest sense, think. We are asked to rate our interactions with online sellers, our experiences with staff in retail outlets and other organisations, the food we eat and the places we go (Williamson, 2017). This gives a somewhat illusionary view of a world where feedback is constantly prioritised, engaged with, used to inform evaluations and improve experiences. Technological advances have meant that companies and institutions can gather and access feedback swiftly and efficiently, as well as use the term 'feedback' as an indicator of interest and consumer care. However, the many opportunities to give feedback do not necessarily encourage a developed or nuanced view of feedback; in fact, they distort conceptions of feedback to a series of clicks supporting a reductionist view. Whether this is in fact feedback in its truest sense is open to debate.

Reflections

» How have you engaged with feedback this week? Consider your working and non-working life.

» How many times have you given and received feedback, and what form did this take?

» Did the feedback make any difference?

If we look at the world of education, we can also note how feedback has become something to be prioritised, valued, monitored and invested in. Feedback has been acknowledged as being key to progress (Black and Wiliam, 1998; Mutch, 2003; Orrell, 2006; Kahu, 2008; Hattie, 2009; Hattie and Clarke, 2018) so its prioritisation seems sensible. However, feedback is frequently listed as an area of student discontent in the National Student Survey (NSS) (Boud and Molloy, 2012; Sambell, 2016; Brooks, 2018; McArthur, 2018). Furthermore, feedback can have significant implications on teacher/tutor workload (Mao and Crosthwaite, 2019; Richards and Richardson, 2019), can be misunderstood (Defeyter and McPartlin, 2007) and often goes ignored by the learner (Paterson et al, 2020; Gul et al, 2016; Glover and Brown, 2006). Indeed it appears that the potential of feedback is largely unfulfilled (Clarke, 2003; Crisp, 2007; Johnson et al, 2016; Molloy and Boud, 2013; Wiliam, 2011; Winstone and Carless, 2019). As such, is feedback really having the desired impact on the learner? Bloxham asserts that feedback has become related to quality assurance and accountability for the benefit of the feedback giver, rather than the learner themselves, which does seem to suggest that the purpose of feedback has been lost in translation. Feedback is clearly an area of policy, practice and the wider discourse that requires further discussion.

Reflection

» How many of the following do you recognise?

− Feedback remains unattended.

− Feedback is not collected.

− Students report not being able to understand feedback.

− Providing feedback has a significant impact on your workload.

As ITE professionals, it could be safe to assume that we understand feedback. We give feedback, receive feedback, teach the value of feedback and educate our student teachers in how to administer feedback in the classroom. It could be argued that feedback operates at a meta-level – we even give feedback on student teacher feedback or indeed the response of the pupils to the feedback. However, maybe we overestimate what an initial teacher education programme brings to our student teachers' understanding of feedback? Student teachers certainly do not join us as empty vessels when it comes to feedback. If anything, their time in the education system means they arrive with a degree of expertise, experience and particular understandings. If we are to ensure that our student teachers enter the profession with a sophisticated view of both the theory and practice of feedback, we need to acknowledge their own experiences and understanding of feedback, too. Speaking to student teachers about their experiences is key to this. But is it their experiences as learners, teachers or both that we need to understand?

Student teachers as learners and teachers

Not only do student teachers bring their own expertise, they also occupy a unique position during their time as both a learner and a practising teacher. As Lee and Schallert ask, is a student teacher '*a student or a teacher, or both or neither, at different times?*' (2016a, p 72). This book is, therefore, interested in the duality of feedback for student teachers who conceptualise feedback both as a learner and as a teacher and any identified similarities and differences across these roles. If, as van den Bergh et al assert, '*teachers' own practices and knowledge of feedback practices is an area worthy of further study, particularly teachers' knowledge, concerns, and beliefs with regard to the feedback they give*' (2013, p 357), then this book is timely. It is only by understanding beliefs around feedback that we can adapt our practice to increase the likelihood of feedback leading to progress both in student teachers and the pupils they teach.

Viewing student teachers as learners and teachers may appear uncontroversial, but the degree, or at least nuances, within this is not so clear cut. This in part is due to the substantial changes that have taken place within the sector over recent decades as they have influenced not only how we train teachers for the future but how we understand student teachers themselves.

In 1998 Edwards wrote:

the control of curricula and an emphasis on guaranteeing their delivery became a Government priority ... mentoring ... is being used as just the latest strategy aimed at limiting teacher agency to classroom practice centred on achieving the curricular targets set by Government ... The policy emphasis on the transmission of curricular subject knowledge which drives practices in primary classrooms is paralleled in English and Welsh initial teacher training by Government directives which emphasise student teachers' curriculum subject knowledge.

(DfE, 1993)
(Edwards, 1998, p 49)

More than 20 years on, it is difficult not to respond with '*how little you knew about what was to come*'. For since then ITE in England has undergone significant transformation involving: a proliferation of routes into teaching including school based and apprenticeships; changes to the ITE curriculum; revised Teacher Standards as well as standards for mentors; different inspection frameworks and the consequences these bring to everything else given the increased accountability and performativity culture across sectors. It has certainly not been a quiet few years. What was already complex is now even more so. Indeed van Geert and Steenbeek argue that both definitions of complexity, '*hard to understand, difficult to manage*' and '*a complex dynamic system and its associated properties*' (2014, pp 23–24), can be applied to education and none more so than ITE.

Reflections

» How has understanding of the student teacher changed during your time in the profession?

» Which of the following models of the student teacher do you think applies and to what extent?

- Learner.

- Apprentice.

- Consumer.

- Technician.

- Novice.

- Teacher.

Few would argue with the proposition that 'learning to teach' has remained the key focus of ITE over this time although what this actually means is, and remains, open to different interpretations which will have implications on whether we see feedback as an equal learner and teacher experience.

What is learning to teach?

Arguably it is not just student teachers who are learners and teachers. Indeed *'part of what it means to be human is an ability to teach'* (Cajkler and Wood, 2016, p 15). Furthermore, many other practice-embedded professional programmes (such as health) may argue that their students occupy similarly different roles and deal with complex demands and competencies associated with both the profession and the training institution (Allen et al, 2019). However, the content and assessment (including feedback) of teacher education can result in a *'heightened understanding of teaching and learning'* (Cajkler and Wood, 2016, p 15). Given the changing context over teacher education over the last 20 years, this *'heightened understanding'* has, however, become focused on different things.

Reflections

» When you think of learning to teach, how do you understand the term?

» How do you know when it has happened?

» Is there an endpoint to the process?

The frequent and fundamental changes experienced by ITE over the recent decades, and particularly between 2010 and 2015, could be described as *'persistent turbulence'* (George and Maguire, 2019, p 20). Increased pathways to the profession have led to a fragmented marketplace with a confusing array of routes. Academic skills and knowledge have become ideologically distinct from professional skills and knowledge with school-based training programmes apparently politically prized (Mutton et al, 2017). A closer focus on metrics, league tables and international comparisons has compounded the competence and measurable-based understanding of teaching. Learning to teach could therefore be seen as having developed into learning to comply with regulatory prescribed standards (Allen et al, 2019; Cajkler and Wood, 2016; Dargusch and Charteris, 2018) as ITE has entered *'the age of compliance'* (Groundwater-Smith and Mockler, 2009, cited in Dargussh and Charteris, 2018, p 26). In England, the prescribed standards for both student teachers and practising teachers are the 2012 Teacher Standards (DfE, 2012). They detail the core competencies associated with eight areas of teaching (including assessment and feedback) as well as professional behaviours and expectations. As Ball (2003) states, *'what it means to teach and what it means to be a teacher (a researcher, an academic) are subtly but decisively changed in the processes of reform'* (p 218). Political and policy changes have, to some extent, reimagined what it is to teach and what it is to learn to teach and, of course, the same will be true of what feedback is within ITE.

Of course, compliance is not exclusive to ITE: under the umbrella of the 'Quality' agenda, it has influenced all sectors of education. As Flores (2020) points out, the lack of a universally agreed definition of quality means that narrow and reductive forms have merged that are easier to identify and perform to. High stakes performance indicators mean that the consequential focus will be on teaching (rather than learning to teach) to the standards, and indeed, the standards associated with assessment and feedback. In other words, *'student teachers are consequently obliged to function as teachers as soon as they are launched into classroom life'* (Edwards, 1998, p 59). Arguably then, learning to teach could be seen as a reductive process; if teaching is a technical exercise then learning to teach is simply a question of being trained to repeat the exercise. Here we see why many teacher educators object to the term *teacher trainer* rather than teacher educator (Lofthouse, 2018). In terms of feedback the implication is that student teachers can be trained to administer the feedback process and repeat it with the learners they encounter. As this book will argue though, it is very difficult to see feedback in a reductive sense; it is messy, complex and unpredictable.

Having said that, the move towards Master's level study in English postgraduate teacher education programmes could be seen as reframing learning to teach again by accentuating the learning. In University-centred routes, student teachers are encouraged to engage with research projects and findings (Flores, 2018) and both the Core Content Framework (Department for Education, 2019b), Early Careers Framework (Department for Education, 2019a) and the 2020 Ofsted inspection framework (Ofsted, 2020) highlight the need to refer to up-to-date research. The fact that the Core Content Framework (Department for Education, 2019b) specifically lists the research that should be used does not, however, suggest teacher, or indeed, researcher autonomy.

Korthagen (2010) argues that reflection and perception are key in learning to be a teacher as does Ellis who notes that privileging 'experience per se' fails to *'take into account either the nature of what beginning teachers learn from experience or the social situation of that learning'* (Ellis, 2010, cited in Mutton et al, 2017, p 15). Lee and Schallert emphasise the learning element in teaching further by stating that learning to teach includes *'multiple and complex forms of learning'* which enable student teachers to *'think, know, feel and act like a teacher* (2016, p 72). It seems, therefore, that learning to teach involves both learning and teaching in complex ways and that student teachers inhabit both of these roles (Hamodi et al, 2017; Lee and Schallert, 2016). Their understanding of feedback will therefore be informed by both of these roles and the experiences within them.

Reflection

»   Nilsson (2008) uses the phrase *'learning to teach and teaching to learn'* to describe teacher education. To what extent does your teacher education programme allow for both of these?

To teach is to learn

Benè and Bergus use the Japanese proverb *'to teach is to learn'* (2014, p 783) in reference to ITE, and it seems pertinent here too as, although this chapter has argued that, despite political and policy changes, teaching and learning are still key to teacher education, maybe the distinction is actually overblown. Are we really able to separate the two (van Geert and Steenbeek, 2014), as doesn't all teaching involve learning as well?

Ell et al's (2017) study found that the greatest influence on learning about teaching was actually teaching. Even experienced teachers are continually learning as they teach whether it be about individual pupils' learning needs, pedagogical approaches or emerging misconceptions. The reflective and reflexive nature of teaching means that teachers are learners too. Indeed, learning to teach does not stop once a student teacher achieves Qualified Teacher Status; in many ways it is just the beginning (Darling-Hammond, 2017). The skills and knowledge learned within a teacher education programme continue to influence practice in future years (Grossman et al, 2000), as a teacher moves from learning to teach to teaching to learn (Lee and Schallert, 2016). Continued professional development and other learning opportunities are seen as synonymous with professionalism; not only is ongoing learning encouraged, it is a core expectation. Furthermore as teachers, our experiences as learners influence what we understand by learning and how we subsequently teach (Hamodi et al, 2017). For student teachers and practising teachers, the relationship between learning and teaching might be blurred, complicated and open to influence from the sociopolitical climate, but it is a relationship that exists nonetheless.

Reflections

Think back over the last week.

»   List your teaching experiences.

»   List your learning experiences.

»   Notice when teaching experiences were also learning experiences.

If we agree that being a student teacher involves being both a learner and a teacher, this book therefore seeks to explore feedback by considering:

» how feedback is understood and experienced by student teachers as learners;

» how feedback is understood by student teachers as practising teachers;

» how these understandings influence one another;

» how understandings of feedback are presented in literature in the contexts of higher education, school education and ITE;

» our own reflections on practice.

WHAT DO WE MEAN BY FEEDBACK?

Before we go further, it is wise to explore what is meant by feedback. Having said that, as the book discusses different understandings (and therefore definitions) of feedback, offering a fixed definition is somewhat problematic. As a result, a particularly broad definition of feedback is offered here, one that does not discount others. Butler and Winnie describe feedback as:

information with which a learner can confirm, add to, overwrite, tune, or restructure information in memory, whether that information is domain knowledge, metacognitive knowledge, beliefs about self and tasks, or cognitive tactics and strategies.

(1995, p 275)

Similarly, Brummer and Kostons state that feedback is '*information regarding aspects of one's performance or understanding, provided by an agent*' (2018, p 1258). A more recent iteration of the term is 'feedforward', but this is avoided here as it carries particular pedagogical connotations which will be discussed in later chapters.

Using these definitions allows for variation in understanding and recognises how the meaning of feedback has changed over time (Dawson et al, 2018). As will be discussed in later chapters, feedback can be defined and understood in many different ways with competing conceptions coexisting.

Reflections

» Write a brief definition of feedback as you understand it.

» Does your definition include references to:

- learner?

- teacher?

- — change?
- — practice?
- — policy?
  » How might your experiences have informed this definition?

The underlying research project

The book has emerged from a phenomenographic PhD study which explored student teacher conceptions of feedback. The study was longitudinal and took place over three years, working with a group of participants over the course of their undergraduate ITE primary programme. There were eight participants altogether, and each was interviewed twice a year about their experiences and understandings of feedback. Open-ended interviews were scheduled around university and placement assessment periods in order to encourage the participants to consider feedback both as a learner and a practising teacher. For each of these, the participants brought with them an artefact that they felt represented feedback. These included filmed lessons from school placement, examples of written feedback provided by the student teacher to pupils in their class or written feedback provided by tutors to the student teacher following academic work. Each interview was transcribed and then analysed using a phenomenographic outcome space. An outcome space is a structure that enables data to be classified in a differentiated way; in this case, participant comments were classified according to both what was learned (understandings of feedback) and how it was learned (as a learner or teacher). This process allowed for the identification of the themes discussed within this text. Ethical guidelines were adhered to throughout. There were particular ethical considerations given to data from school placement.

Book outline

The book is organised into six chapters. Chapter 1 offers an introduction to both the book and English ITE. Chapter 2 outlines some of the key literature that exists around feedback with reference to the three contexts student teachers inhabit: higher education, school education and ITE. The next chapters focus on particular lenses through which we can understand feedback: pedagogical, relational and moral. Lastly, the concluding chapter looks at the implications of the previous findings on practice across educational sectors. Each chapter includes critical issues, an 'in a nutshell' summary and also reflection points for the reader to consider their own understandings and related practice of feedback.

IN A **NUTSHELL**

This chapter has proposed that:

- feedback surrounds us;

- there are difficulties with both the understanding and practice of feedback;

- the ITE context has undergone considerable change in the last 30 years;

- this will have influenced how we understand teacher education and the balance between learning and teaching in relation to feedback;

- student teachers (and indeed teachers) are both learners and teachers, and it is often difficult to separate learning from teaching when it comes to feedback.

REFLECTIONS ON **CRITICAL ISSUES**

Although feedback has become part of life and is a central feature of educational discourse, it is fraught with difficulties which ultimately mean the promise of feedback may remain unfulfilled. This in itself is a justification of this text, but the focus on student teachers is particularly pertinent given that their understandings of feedback will consequently inform their pupils' understanding of feedback.

The neoliberal agenda has resulted in all education sectors rethinking what is understood by and measured as effective teaching and learning, including feedback. Within ITE this has resulted in also rethinking what learning to teach consists of and the best way to achieve predetermined quality professional standards. Whilst this has undoubtedly influenced the extent to which student teachers are viewed as learners and teachers, it is also clear that they, and indeed all teachers, continue to learn to teach and teach to learn throughout their time in the classroom. Experiences and understandings of feedback as a teacher and learner will therefore coexist and influence one another. If the potential of feedback is to be met, we need to understand, reflect upon and redress the feedback narrative by fully understanding the lived feedback experiences of student teachers in both of these roles.

CRITICAL ISSUES

This chapter explores the following critical issues.

- *How do formative assessment and performativity coexist in relation to feedback?*

- *What are the historical and pedagogical roots of feedback?*

- *What are the contextual variations (across differing sectors)?*

- *What is the current position of feedback in initial teacher education?*

Where are we?

Initial teacher education (ITE), like other areas of education, has found itself in somewhat of a feedback frenzy. On the one hand, the sector is aware of the pedagogical purpose and potential of feedback, but on the other, the sector knows that feedback is an area of student dissatisfaction and, as such, has become a key performance metric.

This conflict is arguably felt more acutely in ITE than in any other area of higher education (HE). Not only are student teachers asked about their own experiences of feedback within their training, they also have to give feedback to the pupils they teach and will need to meet particular standards in this area to pass the course. Initial teacher educators will both judge the quality of the student teacher feedback and be judged by the student teachers in the feedback they give; feedback appears to have a stranglehold in all the facets of ITE.

Reflections

» Consider how many times the term or practice of 'feedback' comes into your work. Include:

- your own teaching and assessment practice;

- the content of your teaching;

- placement experiences;

- quality assurance processes;

- use of sector metrics;

- improvement of planning processes and subject development.

» Do all of these encounters imply the same conception of feedback?

To explore the contextual complexities further, this chapter outlines the key changes in policy and practice across HE, school education and ITE, and argues that these can be grouped into differing conceptions of feedback. However, it begins by situating feedback within the broader assessment discourse, which has seen the emergence of two central ideas: formative assessment and performativity. In ITE these are often not natural bedfellows, appearing to almost represent pedagogy and performance.

And how did we get here?

The opposing views of assessment

It is difficult to explore conceptions of feedback without situating these within the assessment. This task has a historical and conceptual dimension, as not only can assessment be seen as 'a dangerously ambiguous concept' (Broadfoot, 1999, p 3); a study of the last few decades indicates that assessment consists of broadly *two* ambiguous and diametrically opposed concepts: assessment *for* learning, or formative assessment, and assessment *of* learning, or summative assessment, which is increasingly linked to performativity. The uncomfortable coexistence of these two concepts has led to dubious practice, misconceptions and unhelpful, value-laden polarisation for both assessment and feedback.

A look through the educational history books reveals how these conceptions developed. In England, the Great Education Debate of the 1970–80s saw the beginnings of a new educational discourse, where 'reasonable standards [and] expectations' (Department of Education and Science, 1980) started to be emphasised. The year 1988 marked one of the most substantial pieces of education legislation with the introduction of a statutory national system of pupil assessment, which had far-reaching consequences, not just for the education system but also for how that system was monitored, controlled and evidenced for the newly empowered stakeholders such as parents (Daugherty, 2004). The introduction of league tables in 1992 and the many versions of progress measures that followed (value added in 2002, contextual value added in 2006, expected progress in 2011 and more recently 'progress 8' scores in 2016), combined with an increasingly high-stakes inspection framework, resulted in assessment being used to identify underperformance (Leckie and Goldstein, 2017). Feedback sat within this shift, acting as an assessment tool. As a result, over time assessment standards became no longer a standard to be reached but the standard to be exceeded if a school was to compete in this brave new world (Broadfoot, 2007), a world where an assessment was a measurable and comparable mark of competence whether for a learner, teacher or school. We are now in a position where feedback itself is not only a tool for assessment but is a measure itself: Have we given enough feedback? Is it having the desired effect? Are learners happy with the quality and quantity of feedback they receive?

By the beginning of the twenty-first century, England arguably developed an education system that was:

not only as tightly controlled and centrally directed as any in the world ... but also a system that might appear ... to be infected by a kind of madness [because of the] rampant growth of a forest of assessment procedures which threatens to throttle the whole education system within a dense canopy of externally imposed performance indicators.

(Broadfoot, 1999, p 3)

Reflections

» How does your own feedback practice reflect Broadfoot's assertion regarding 'externally imposed performance indicators'?

  – Is your feedback practice measured and tracked?

  – Is this in reference to quantity, quality or both?

  – How are these values defined and by whom?

» As an ITE practitioner, do you impose additional performance indicators related to the feedback of the students you teach? How much voice do you have in this?

Contradictorily, the same period saw the emergence of conflicting thinking about assessment and feedback within policymaking (Daugherty, 2004), a conception that was formative, self-regulatory and learner focused. Formative assessment was developed from Scriven's (1967) *'formative evaluation'*, but it was the work of Black and Wiliam in their influential report *'Inside the Black Box'* (1998) that really brought it to prominence. Black and Wiliam identified the consequential nature of formative assessment *'when the evidence is actually used to adapt the teaching work to meet the needs'* (Black and Wiliam, 1998, p 2) of the learner. In other words, for assessment to be formative, judgements should be used to influence future learning and teaching.

In terms of summative assessment, it is perhaps easier to spot the influence of this as the summative assessment is now seen as a performance measure; education is now a world where university, school and individual improvement are measured through performance marks and grades (Beaumont, O'Doherty and Shannon, 2011). In HE, providers are also judged according to the assessment questions within the National Student Survey (NSS) and the loaded assessment processes and systems that need to be complied with are *'inconsistent with [the more formative] pedagogic criteria'* (Ali, Ahmed and Rose, 2017, pp 246–47). The growth of an education culture focused on external performance testing, and accountability has perpetuated the confusion between the value attached to formative processes and summative judgements; national assessment systems appear to be more valued by the system and have more significance (Harlen, 2004; Black and Wiliam, 2014; DeLuca et al, 2012). Brooks (2018) makes a wider point that within HE, students are increasingly viewed as customers (Leach, 2019) who are entitled to a good assessment and feedback experience; therefore providers need to keep students satisfied and enrolled and need to compete with other providers using performance data. Within ITE, the school context is also relevant as student teachers soon realise that summative standards result in a higher league table position for the school.

Despite the apparent influence of formative assessment in policy and practice, the simultaneous growth of performativity, and the ongoing divergence between the two ideas, has meant that the purposes, expectations and practice of assessment and feedback have become distorted; performance data, used for governance purposes, has become prioritised and ideas subsequently polarised. As a result, given that feedback is a key part of formative assessment, it too has associated conceptions that do not necessarily align, perceptions of 'effectiveness' that are disputed and difficulties with principles being turned into over-simplified practice. As Clarke asserts, *'feedback is the central theme of formative assessment, yet it is the element most laden with a legacy of bad practice and misguided views'* (2003, p 3).

Reflection

» Consider the feedback expectations and practices within your own ITE provider. To what extent are these expectations related to:

 — a formative conception of assessment/feedback?

 — a performativity-focused concept of assessment/feedback where feedback needs to be accounted for, complied with and is seen as a mark of 'quality'?

The impact on feedback

We can see the beginnings of a formative understanding of feedback in Ramaprasad's seminal work of 1983. Borrowing an analogy from engineering, formative feedback was redefined as *'information about the gap between the actual level and the reference level of a system parameter which is used to alter the gap in some way'* (Ramaprasad, 1983, p 4). Within heating systems, feedback is *'the discrepancy between the current state and the desired state'*, and for it to be formative there needs to be *'a mechanism within the feedback loop to bring the current state closer to the desired state'* (Wiliam, 2011, p 121). This presents rather a mechanistic approach to feedback as something that will fix a gap in understanding. Given the professional expectations to 'fix' learning gaps and evidence 'good' practice quickly, formative feedback has also been recast into formulaic strategies such as the feedback sandwich (Boud and Molloy, 2012). The feedback sandwich is a metaphor for placing the 'negative' comment in between two 'positive' comments. In this context, 'negative' is seen as synonymous with constructive or developmental. The association of constructive as negative is interesting in itself.

Feedback is actually far more difficult and complex than it appears (Wiliam, 2011) and cannot be reduced to a generalised 'good' practice or strategy. ITE educators will recognise this as they have had to respond to top-down strategies from either central government or their own HE institution, but also have some responsibility for encouraging particular strategies with the student teachers who are also influenced by the contextual practice of school placement. ITE educators will therefore feel the influence of strategies from all directions whilst still seeking to develop reflective, critical and analytical teachers for the future. As Sadler states:

at the risk of glossing over the complexities of what is known about feedback, the general picture is that the relationship between its form, timing and effectiveness is complex and variable, with no magic formulas.

(Sadler, 2010, p 536)

Reflections

» How has feedback been translated into a particular strategy or practice within your experience? Consider:

- the strategies the student teachers experience in school;
- how evidencing the Teacher Standards encourages/discourages a formulaic approach;
- the top-down strategies presented (or encouraged) from HE or central government.

» To what extent do you think these encourage a 'complex and variable' understanding of the phenomenon of feedback?

Contextual variation

Not only have the two broad conceptions of formative assessment and performativity influenced how feedback is understood and practised, literature suggests that feedback is understood differently in different contexts. ITE combines two contexts, HE and school education, and subsequently has its own context. Evidence from these differing contexts further supports the varied complexity of feedback.

Higher education

The HE context does not present a clear-cut view of feedback. Initially, conceptions of feedback tended to be rooted in Ramaprasad's (1983) view of feedback as closing a gap. Sadler's (1989) work extended this idea by identifying three conditions of feedback:

1. an understanding of the next learning goal;
2. an understanding of current learning and the gap between the two;
3. how to close the gap.

The closure of a learning gap supports the understanding of formative feedback as having a consequence. Indeed, it is possible to see here how feedback began to be referred to as 'feedforward' as it needed to inform future learning and teaching. Sadler's (1989) work was also important because it suggested that the learner had a role in the process. This learner centricity was in opposition to a, perhaps more traditional, view where feedback needs to be delivered by a more knowledgeable other or, in other words, a teacher-centric understanding where feedback is '*telling*' (Boud and Molloy, 2012, p 14). Nicol and Macfarlane-Dick's (2004b) model took this further by placing the learner at the centre and associating it with self-regulated learning or 'learnacy' (Butler and Winne, 1995). In this model, the learner holds the central active role in the feedback process, '*actively construct[ing] his/her own understanding of feedback messages*' (Nicol and Macfarlane-Dick, 2004a, p 201).

Winstone (2018) furthered this by recognizing two feedback paradigms within higher education: the old and the new. Here we see that an example of value-laden polarisation as 'new' can be interpreted as 'better'. The old paradigm reflects a 'teacher-centric' model of feedback, and the new paradigm is 'learner-centric' where the learner needs to not only undergo a '*conceptual change*' in thinking (Black and Wiliam, 2014, p 28) but is also an active decision-maker, identifying, engaging with and actioning feedback; the learner is an '*active agent*' (Espasa and Martinez-Melo, 2019, p 111) and '*drive[s] feedback for themselves*' (Evans, 2016, p 5). Arguably this is aspirational given the top-down education system that currently exists in many countries. Furthermore, there is increasing evidence that feedback practice remains resolutely transmissive and summative (Nicol, 2010; Ali, Ahmed and Rose, 2017; Winstone, 2018). Molloy and Boud (2013) identify two nostrums that have contributed to the unremitting 'old' paradigm in HE: all feedback is good feedback, and with feedback, the more the merrier. The massification of HE has also influenced the way feedback is understood. Larger classes, closer scrutiny of quality processes and the impact of time/workload pressures have resulted in the potential for feedforward becoming incongruent with current assessment procedures (Ali, Ahmed and Rose, 2017). Increased accountability has led to a reframing of feedback. Carless (2015) calls this '*double feedback duty*', where feedback is not only driving a pedagogical need for the learner but also meets the requirements of 'quality' surveillance processes.

Reflection

» Identify an aspect of your own feedback practice (eg written feedback, school experience feedback). Does it encourage:

  – a teacher-centric approach where the teacher is the holder of knowledge and feedback is telling?

  – a learner-centric approach where the learner is active agent and decision-maker?

In addition, within the HE sector there is strong evidence that students are dissatisfied with their feedback experience. Yang and Carless (2013) and Beaumont, O'Doherty and Shannon (2011) argue that this is partly because students find the experience of feedback in HE less supportive than their pre-course school experience. Depressingly, student perceptions of feedback appear to decrease as they progress across the three years of a standard undergraduate course (Ali, Ahmed and Rose, 2017). The National Student Survey data supports this by identifying assessment and feedback as the least satisfactory aspect of the HE experience (Beaumont, O'Doherty and Shannon, 2011; Yang and Carless, 2013). This has led many HE institutions to conclude that students are not interested in feedback (Sambell, Gibson and Montgomery, 2007) or are not clear about what constitutes feedback (Adcroft, 2011), which in itself does imply rather a teacher-centric understanding where the learners have a deficit (Boud and Molloy, 2012) and are not able to recognise feedback when they see it.

School education

The school education discourse appears to agree with Black and Wiliam (1998) that feedback is key to progress. Hattie (2003) found that feedback resulted in a significant 'effect size' and the ongoing meta-analysis of the Education Endowment Fund (The Sutton Trust, 2020) continued to identify feedback as having the potential for high learning impact. Notwithstanding the power and influence of summative assessment within the school sector, feedback is generally seen as formative and leading to consequence (Hattie and Clarke, 2018).

Existing school sector feedback research is often focused on the effectiveness of particular strategies. There is less on how teachers, and indeed pupils, conceptualise feedback (Brown, 2011). The research that does exist in this area often identifiers of a mismatch between espoused conceptions and the translation to practice (Dixon, Hawe and Parr, 2011). In terms of the roles of teacher and pupil, school-based feedback literature does seem to identify that both have a part to play, although this is not necessarily equitable. Indeed, as with higher education, feedback is largely seen as a 'gift from teacher to pupil' (Hargreaves, 2005, p 6). Policy literature reinforces this further by detailing teachers' professional responsibilities in relation to feedback. The English National Teachers' Standards (DfE, 2012, p 12), by which both student and qualified teachers are judged, state that teachers must, as a key requirement, 'give pupils regular feedback, both orally and through accurate marking, and encourage pupils to respond to the feedback' (DfE, 2012, p 12). Although both pupils and teachers have a role to play, it is teachers who are ultimately responsible for both of these duties being completed.

Although some school literature appears to support the development of independent and self-directed learners (Kirton et al, 2007; Hargreaves, 2013) through feedback (Butler and Winne, 1995; Black and Wiliam, 1998), many school-based practices further reinforce the conception that the teacher is central and in control. Brown (2011) argues that teachers' conceptions are developed through their own experiences of the particular phenomenon. In other words, how teachers understand feedback, and the role they take, will depend on how they have experienced feedback as a learner. If their experiences have emphasised that the teacher has ultimate responsibility for feedback, this is the role they will inhabit as a student teacher. This therefore makes the feedback practices within ITE particularly significant.

Reflection

» Practitioners in ITE will explore 'good' feedback with student teachers. Does this translate to the feedback we practise ourselves?

Of course, if learners are to be more central in the feedback process, there will be implication for the role of the teacher. Learners will not necessarily be able to grasp the role from the start and will benefit from careful modelling, scaffolding and support (Brown, Harris and Harnett, 2012) to develop the appropriate autonomous skills (Hargreaves, 2013). The Teachers' Standards support the view that the teacher is somehow responsible for learner independence and autonomy, stating that teachers need to 'encourage pupils to respond to the feedback' (DfE, 2012, p 12).

Peterson and Irving (2008) found that secondary-aged children conceptualised feedback as a consequential process but also that the likelihood of this feedback being used was dependent on whether the learner was performance orientated or not. A 'good' performance resulted in a positive response to the feedback, and a 'poor' performance caused the feedback to be viewed negatively and possibly ignored (Peterson and Irving, 2008). This seems to indicate that the constructiveness or usefulness of feedback is indeed in the eye of the beholder as school-aged learners interpret feedback in different ways (Sambell and McDowell, 1998). The implication is that the focus should not necessarily be on the feedback itself but on how it is received by the learner (Gamlem and Munthe, 2014).

There is also evidence to suggest that primary school teachers conceptualise feedback, particularly praise, as motivation (Murtagh, 2014), although Brown et al's research (2012) indicates that this conception is in relation to learning rather than well-being. However, praise is not necessarily a good thing and is also open to differing understanding and ultimately practice. In fact, teacher praise could have a negative impact in that it would reduce the necessity for intrinsic motivation; this would further reinforce the view that the teacher is in control of the learning process (Murtagh, 2014). Generic and non-targeted praise is seen as ineffective (Hattie and Timperley, 2007) but nevertheless appears to be favoured most with school teachers (Burnett and Mandel, 2010).

More recently there has been a further change in the school sector. In response to issues relating to teacher retention and recruitment, Ofsted (Office for Standards in Education, Children's Services and Skills) offered 'myth-busting guidance' on marking and feedback, stating:

Ofsted recognises that marking and feedback to pupils, both written and oral, are important aspects of assessment. However, Ofsted does not expect to see any specific frequency, type or volume of marking and feedback.

(Ofsted, 2018)

This followed the findings of the Teacher Workload report (Department for Education, 2016) that made a link between the accountability agenda and the myth of more (and detailed) feedback as good practice (Winstone, 2018). There appears to be something of a pendulous nature to what is perceived to be good or bad practice over the years, and marking is a pertinent example. Changing the value of practice so frequently, and in such a polarised manner, does not support solid conceptions of learning, particularly when they are coupled with surveillance. Alderton (2019) argues the school assessment system has over-normalised certain values and behaviours, allowing for the 'new regimes of truth' (p 1). These 'truths' are difficult to change as teachers often become embedded in the surveillance of the perceived normalised practice. As such, it is difficult to see how a change of direction from Ofsted will result in swift meaningful changes to understanding and values.

Initial teacher education

ITE combines HE and school-based education. Arts, Jaspers and Joosten-ten Brinke (2016) highlight how significant teacher education is in the development of feedback stating that:

it is of eminent importance to ... reflect on the different types of feedback that are used and on their effectiveness. Moreover, it is worthwhile to reflect on the way of giving feedback with colleagues and with students, especially with students in teacher training institutes who have to be trained in providing feedback themselves.

(Arts, Jaspers and Joosten-ten Brinke, 2016, p 171)

Given this assertion, the dearth of feedback research for this group of students is somewhat alarming. Furthermore, the research that does exist does not really consider the unique position these students are in as both receivers and givers of feedback. There are studies (Poskitt, 2014; Xu and Brown, 2016) that have explored the necessary features of assessment literacies needed within professional training programmes, but these do not always make specific reference to feedback. The research that does exist into the development of student teachers is often from outside the UK and looks at a broader understanding of teaching and learning (Donche and Van Petegem, 2009; Cheng, Tang and Cheng, 2014) although, of course, feedback is positioned within this. There is more research on self-regulation (Endedijk et al, 2014), but this does not explicitly deal with how feedback can support its development. Furthermore, there is very little research that focuses on the unique position of student teachers as both learners and teachers. Endedijk and Vermunt support this oversight stating, 'studies on how student teachers regulate their learning during teaching practice and on how they regulate learning from both theory and practice in parallel, are almost absent' (2014, p 1119).

Research also supports the point that teachers' conceptions are a product of the beliefs they develop as a student (Strijbos and Ufer, 2019), implying that understandings (or indeed misunderstandings) are transferred and repeated. Carless and Boud (2018, p 1316) describe these beliefs as often 'limited absolutist' in nature. However, Cheng, Cheng and Tang (2010) argue that student teachers see their teacher educators as role models they can learn from; modelling of behaviours by teacher educators can inform student teachers' own understanding and practice. Therefore, ITE can impact student teacher beliefs irrespective of their pre-course experience and has a key role in feedback practice in the future.

Colleagues from ITE would probably agree that the sector is rich in feedback opportunities given the combination of academic and placement assessments. A key source of feedback within such programmes will be the school mentors who support student teachers on school placement. Kwan and Lopez-Real (2005, p 275) found that mentors identified '*provider of feedback*' (p 275) as one of the most important aspects of their role. However, that paper also suggests that the role of a mentor is conflicted between supporting student teachers (through feedback) and assessing performance as part of quality assurance (Kwan and Lopez-Real, 2005). Here we see the pedagogical and performative conflict once more.

The lack of research into feedback and ITE may go some way to explaining its identification as a priority within the 2015 Carter Review of Initial Teacher Training in England. The report recommended feedback should be focused on student teacher outcomes, be goal oriented and encourage student teachers to engage with feedback independently and professionally. In terms of school pupils, the only reference is for student teachers to know '*how to give effective feedback and the next steps for progression*' (Carter, 2015, p 33). The report also acknowledges that Teachers' Standard 6 (Assessment) is a weakness in student teacher outcomes: '*of all areas of ITT content, we believe the most significant improvements are needed on training for assessment*' (Carter, 2015, pp 54–55). It seems strange that there is very little advice on how teacher educators could improve the feedback practice and understanding of the student teachers themselves.

By examining the historical and contextual understandings of feedback, this chapter has argued that there are both parallel and conflicting conceptions of feedback. As ITE straddles contexts, it is influenced by both HE and the school sector. When the duality of student teachers as both learners and teachers is also factored in, it is not hard to see why ITE could consider itself to be at the centre of the feedback maze. This book examines the understandings of feedback articulated by student teachers themselves in an attempt to unpick just how feedback is understood within ITE.

IN A **NUTSHELL**

This chapter has argued that:

- ITE navigates conflicting purposes, formats and understandings of feedback;

- the sector is dealing with the two opposing concepts of assessment, summative (used for performative purposes) and formative, both of which influence feedback;

- there is a tendency within education to strategize feedback into simplistic and formulaic approaches;

- ITE represents the interface between HE and the school sector, each of which, literature suggests, understands and practises feedback in different ways;

- if ITE is to develop reflective, critical practitioners who are agents of change, we need to explore the complexity of feedback further by helping student teachers reflect on their conscious beliefs.

REFLECTIONS ON **CRITICAL ISSUES**

Feedback fills a unique and significant position in ITE, given that it has been a key feature of policy, practice, standards and performance measures across HE and schools. It has historical and pedagogical roots in the formative assessment movement but has also become a key feature of performativity. These two coexist uncomfortably and rather contradictorily, given that they have been informed by very different ideologies. Given that ITE effectively straddles HE and the school sector, the contextual variation across these sectors complicates conceptions of feedback even further and there is often a disconnect between what is viewed as pedagogically appropriate and quality assured.

CHAPTER 3 | PEDAGOGICAL UNDERSTANDINGS OF FEEDBACK

The next three chapters use student teacher comments to discuss possible understandings of feedback with pedagogical, relational and moral dimensions.

CRITICAL ISSUES

This chapter explores the following critical issues:

- *what is meant by the pedagogical discourses evident in feedback;*
- *feedback as a deficit;*
- *feedback as a gift;*
- *feedback as a cycle;*
- *feedback as 'learnacy'.*

Pedagogical discourse

Pedagogical understandings can be seen as a currency of ideas or conceptions associated with learning and teaching. These can be developed over time, exchanged with others and often adapted for differing contexts. For student teachers, exchanges take place in multiple ways:

- » tutor and student teacher;
- » mentor and student teacher;
- » class teacher and student teacher;
- » student teacher and student teacher;
- » lastly, student teacher and pupil.

This can be expanded even further to include the student teachers' pre-course experiences of learning, all of which are likely to include ideas about pedagogy.

This chapter explores how feedback can be conceptualised through a pedagogical lens. To do this, the chapter refers to some of the existing pedagogical discourses around feedback. Pedagogical discourse may be defined as 'the operation of a set of principles by which *persons are apprenticed into ways of working valued in a culture*' (Christie, 1995, p 221). Those apprenticed '*both participate in the construction of the discourse … [and] are shaped by it*' (Christie, 1995, p 221). In other words, pedagogical discourse is much more than language in use but refers to what is seen as legitimate, normalised knowledge, which is privileged by those who are perceived to have power (Bernstein, 2004; see also Winter and Linehan, 2014). If we apply this to teacher education, certain pedagogical discourses will be legitimised by others, for example, mentors and tutors, which will influence the reproduction of the discourses within the student teachers. Discourses within legislation, standards and inspection criteria will further reinforce what is viewed as pedagogically appropriate and valued. Furthermore, given the pedagogical focus of teacher educators, part of the content of student teachers' education is highly likely to include exploration and reflection in relation to these discourses. The student teacher data used within this chapter has therefore been analysed and aligned with particular existing discourses around feedback: feedback as a deficit, feedback as a gift, feedback as a cycle and feedback as 'learnacy'.

Reflection

»   Reflect on your own teaching on feedback as well as the assessments the students complete. Are any particular feedback discourses highlighted as preferred?

Discourse 1: feedback as a deficit

The first discourse is feedback as a deficit or, to be more exact, feedback to close a perceived deficit in the learner. Although sometimes implicit, some student teachers suggest that the role of feedback is to 'fix' or close a gap in learning; this can be in their role as learner and teacher. We can see evidence of this in the participants referred to within this text. As a learner, Lilly stated that she felt the purpose of feedback was related to progression so the targets were very important. She uses the word 'weakness' to imply the deficit identified and also stated that engaging with the identified deficit made the difference; gaps in learning are seen as weaknesses that require fixing by both learner and teacher.

Lilly: I think it is a key aspect within progression because I think if I was to hand in that piece of work and I were to get no feedback back, and then I went to hand in another piece of work, I wouldn't have known where to kind of improve … I'd have no indication on where my strengths were or where my weaknesses lie, and so how am I meant to … progress forward?

Lilly recognises what Hattie states are the key feedback questions '*where am I going?*', '*how am I going?*', '*where to next?*' (2009, p 177; see also Sadler, 1989). Both sources link to the discourse of 'closing the gap' which developed from the work of Ramaprasad (1983). Given that closing the gap is a metaphor where feedback is '*the discrepancy between the current state and the desired state*' and is only relevant if there is '*a mechanism within the feedback loop to bring the current state closer to the desired state*' (Wiliam, 2011, p 121), there is already a problematic disconnect with reducing something as complex as feedback to a mechanical procedure. It assumes that feedback is simple; once feedback is provided, the learning step is completed. Feedback is far from linear but is dynamic, fluid, with both predicted and unpredicted consequences. Furthermore, another potential difficulty is that often the deficit (or gap) is identified by another, therefore implicitly supporting a teacher-centric view of feedback. Deficits identified by the learner may well be more relevant.

Reflection

» When giving written feedback to students, how does the form and content of your feedback suggest that feedback is a deficit? For example, does the structure of the feedback sheet identify gaps and ways to close them? If so, is there any opportunity for students to be involved in identifying these gaps?

Further, student teacher comments suggest that the perceived purpose of feedback is identifying a weakness or lack of something.

Evie: We didn't receive any feedback until it was submitted … it wasn't sort of next steps … so it was less maybe like developmental.

This is also true in the role of teacher.

Evie: Then I also think it's important that the children know where they are and how they can improve, because that's so frustrating to want to be progressing but not knowing how to sort of, how to get there next.

It is interesting to note in the above example that Evie implies the learners are reliant on the teacher/tutor identifying both the gap and the action, rather than the learner doing it themselves. This is in contrast to much of the literature that applies Ramaprasad's (1983) and Sadler's (1989) gap analogy to the learner; that is, the learner identifies and closes the gap (Clarke, 2003; Hattie and Clarke, 2018; Savvidou, 2018). Zhang and Zheng (2018) propose a slightly different model where responsibilities are shared between learner and teacher: teachers identify the deficit, provide feedback to the learner and then encourage learners to close the gap. This better represents the conceptions expressed by many student teachers when they describe their actions as a teacher.

Reflection

» Can students in higher education or pupils in schools ever be wholly responsible for identifying their own learning gaps? What would this mean for the role of the tutor/teacher?

The identification of the teacher's role within the idea of deficit may be a consequence of the way that 'closing the gap' has become central to educational policy over the last 15 years across both the higher education and school sectors (Clarke, 2003; Nicol and Macfarlane-Dick, 2006; Hattie, 2009; Black and Wiliam, 2014; Clarke, 2014; Evans, 2016; Hattie and Clarke, 2018). Schools in England are encouraged to identify and close the gap between different groups of learners and are judged (by Ofsted) on their ability to do so (Laws, 2013; Rea, Hill and Dunford, 2013; Wilson, 2014; Andrews, Robinson and Hutchinson, 2017). In this way, the deficit discourse has grown beyond feedback to become central to a teacher's and school's purpose and is seen as a measure of effectiveness. As part of this, identified published strategies support the notion that the deficit is fixable and within the power of the teacher/school (Sharples et al, 2011), usually through strategies that offer a quick fix approach.

Reflections

» How does higher education, initial teacher education and/or school policy and practice buy into the idea that the identification and closing of learning gaps is a simple, linear process?

» What does this simplified process fail to take account of?

Wiliam (2011) states fixable gaps or goals need to be 'within reach' but also with a 'degree of challenge' (p 150). If the deficit selected is beyond learner reach, students are likely to disengage. This can be seen in the comments of the student teachers, 'you just pick out one thing; it is small manageable target for them to achieve within the week or a day'. Of course, if the teacher (rather than learner) identifies the gap, no matter how appropriate it is, it is possibly less likely to be engaged with anyway.

Discourse 2: feedback as a gift

Askew and Lodge (2000) acknowledge that conceptualising feedback as a gift from the expert tends to be the dominant discourse in education. Indeed, we see constant reference to 'following expert [mentors, teachers and tutors] input – by taking opportunities to practise, receive feedback and improve' (Department for Education, 2019b, p 9) within the ITT Core Content Framework.

Reflections

» Do you agree that 'feedback as a gift' is the dominant discourse in education?

» Is your answer the same across all sectors of education?

If Askew and Lodge (2000) are correct, it is probably unsurprising then that there is a lot of evidence of this discourse within student teacher comments. Daisy was fairly explicit in her view of the teacher as a bestower of the gift of feedback. As a learner, within the context of a university, Daisy saw the teacher's (or tutor's) role as one of direction; the teacher was the one who *knew*, and this knowledge was *gifted* to the one who did not know.

Daisy: I think most of the feedback role was with the tutor here because he was more knowledgeable than me ... so he could tell me what I needed to do ...

Her comments are supported by Evans (2013), who associates gifting feedback with the teacher as expert who passes on information to a passive recipient, largely through telling or correction. This, of course, can impact how peer feedback is understood.

Daisy: Because in a teaching situation I am the expert, so I know the correct answer in most cases ... so, like when I'm doing maths questions I can give them feedback knowing that I know the answer. Whereas in a peer situation I don't know the best way, so it's more difficult to tell people what to do.

Daisy's comments support a view of learning as transmission, which Esterhazy (2018) argues, is prevalent in education. Transmission implies that knowledge is exchanged from one to another, reflecting the analogy of feedback as a gift. If feedback as a gift is as prevalent as Esterhazy (2018) states, then Daisy would have experienced a transmissive approach in her pre-course schooling. Carless argues students' preferences (and indeed conceptions) of feedback are often because of their previous experience where they have developed *'limited absolutist beliefs about knowledge'* (Carless and Boud, 2018, p 1316).

As a teacher, Sapna also revealed a transmissive view of feedback, but by the end of the project she had reflected upon this and recognised some of the issues with conceptualising feedback this way.

Sapna: I think what I've realised is, I maybe took it for granted that if you put feedback in a book for ... any [pupil], as long as you wrote it in a language they could understand, they would get it. But, I'd be disinclined now to put feedback in any books unless I was writing it next to the child and saying, 'Right, in the next lesson you need to do this. I'm putting this here to remind you.'

This implies that Sapna originally viewed the giving of feedback as more valuable than the receiving of feedback by the pupils. She is describing a model of feedback where the teacher knows what the other needs to do, prescribes what to do and checks the learners have done it. However, Sapna is also now implying a view that takes greater account of how the learner interprets and acts upon the feedback; she is both gifting the feedback and is also aware that the learner is not necessarily passive. She has reflected on the connotations of feedback as a gift in that the implied teacher-centricity results in a degree of complacency; that is, there is nothing wrong with the feedback, it is how it is received that is the problem. As Molloy and Boud put it, *'if only students would listen more attentively then all would be well'* (2013, p 15).

Reflections

» As an ITE professional, you may have provided similar feedback to the same student over time. Where does the fault lie, if indeed, there is any blame?

» Now consider HE discourse in relation to metrics such as the National Student Survey. Are low scores attributed to the quality of teacher or learner?

» Given that feedback appears to be largely teacher-centric, why are issues with feedback sometimes viewed as learner-centric?

Discourse 3: feedback as a cycle

As teachers, many student teachers indicate an understanding of feedback as a consequence-based cycle, reflecting some of the meaning of formative assessment outlined by Black and Wiliam (1998). This is probably not surprising given the reference to formative assessment and feedback within higher education assessment strategies and the Teachers' Standards (DfE, 2012). More recently, the ITT Core Content Framework asserted that *'to be of value, teachers use information from assessments to inform the decisions they make; in turn, pupils must be able to act on feedback for it to have an effect'* and *'high-quality feedback ... is likely to be accurate and clear, encourage further effort, and provide specific guidance on how to improve'* (Department for Education, 2019b, p 23).

Reflection

» In your ITE programme are the formative or summative dimensions of feedback prioritised? Consider both subject content and practice.

As a teacher, Sapna conceptualized feedback as a joint dialogue where gaps were identified and closed in an ongoing cyclical (or looped) manner. She felt that the learner had to have a voice in this process.

Sapna: It's about ... taking the time to make sure that the feedback has been understood, and also exactly what the next step should be, and involving the learner in those next steps so that they come up with a plan ... You come up with a plan together rather than just going 'right there you go, there's your feedback, crack on' ... it's more dialogic. ... it's a cycle ... like a hamster wheel.

Lilly, too, used a similar metaphor to describe feedback.

Lilly: it's not ... about that linear progress. It's more ... a continuum, that circle or a triangle or whatever you want to do, it's just like a continuous thing, like a ball that won't stop rolling.

In addition, student teachers appear to recognise that feedback needed to have a consequence. The consequence was often related to a deficit notion of next steps whereby a gap was identified and then closed. Although literature often presents single models of feedback, here we see that the 'gap' and 'cycle' conceptions are able to coexist. Furthermore, the inclusion of consequential action could represent a learner-centric model of feedback, but actioning feedback could also be a consequence of teacher-centric models of feedback as a gift or telling as well. Although if, as Carless and Boud (2018) suggest, a learner-centric model encourages the learner to direct learning, make sense of the feedback and actually construct knowledge, then it is reasonable to conclude that a teacher-directed feedback cycle will not be as successful. Could this be at the heart of feedback that remains unactioned? The feedback comes from the tutor rather than the learner.

Reflection

» It is likely that at least some of the feedback you give to your students remains unactioned. Consider why this might be. Can/do your students:

- interpret the feedback?

- recognise how to action the feedback?

- identify a range of strategies to do this?

- appreciate the feedback?

Without action, feedback is a linear process resulting in merely *'dangling data'* (Sadler, 1989, p 121) with no consequence. Indeed, Carless argues *'students need to take action to improve because unless comments are taken up, there is minimal value in feedback.'* (Carless, 2018). Nicol and Macfarlane-Dick (2006, p 213) state that the feedback cycle should *'help students to recognise the next steps in learning and how to take them, both during production and in relation to the next [learning].'* Hattie (2009) agrees, describing the subsequent action from feedback as key, while Kahu (2008), citing Gibbs and Simpson (2004), affirms *'feedback must be attended to'* (p 192). Indeed, some would argue that it is the action that actually makes feedback feedback (Ramaprasad, 1983; Sadler, 1989; Boud and Molloy, 2013; Esterhazy, 2018) as it allows the cycle to be closed before it can start again (Reinholz, 2016). If this is the case, maybe some of the time taken on writing unattended to feedback would be better spent on developing feedback literacies with our students (Carless and Boud, 2018).

As teachers, student teachers appear to recognise the feedback cycle, which is unsurprising given that three of the four subsections of Teachers' Standard (TS) 6: Monitoring and Assessment (DfE, 2012) imply a cyclical process where *'formative assessment is used'* to *'set targets, and plan subsequent lessons'* and teachers need to *'encourage pupils to respond to feedback'* (p 12). TS6 is a standard that student teachers will need to evidence if they are to achieve Qualified Teacher Status, so their focus on this discourse is understandable. After all, if you do not 'buy into' the discourse, even superficially, you do not qualify as a teacher.

This in itself reinforces a teacher-centric view of feedback. The standard implies it is the teacher's responsibility to ensure the cycle is completed, not the learner's, and the standards agenda ensures that it is teachers, not learners, who are judged on how formative feedback is. This gives the discourse further value for the teacher. When we situate this within wider higher education feedback discourse, particularly written feedback, we see that student teachers will have a teacher-centric view further reinforced.

Discourse 4: feedback as 'learnacy'

The next section of this chapter focuses on a generally more learner-centric conception of feedback. This is often referred to as '*learnacy*' (Butler and Winne, 1995), synthesising conceptions related to self-regulation, self-efficacy and autonomy where the learner holds an active role. As teachers, developing these skills in our learners means a consequential change to our role and responsibilities. The participants seemed to be aware of this.

Lilly: I want to say that the child does have their own responsibility in it, but then how do they develop that responsibility? Is that for the teacher? I guess to some degree it is ... I think you can still try and encourage but then again, it's hard because there comes to a point where, like I said, only so much a teacher can do.

This indicates that, within the school, Lilly recognised the responsibility of the learner in the feedback process but was unsure of how this influenced the role of the teacher. However, as a student in higher education, Lilly felt that learners developed a greater responsibility as they got older.

Lilly: I do think that changes when you get older. You get to a certain age you're at the point where you make your own decisions and there's only so much a teacher can do.

Similarly, Lottie stated that primary teachers had a greater responsibility to ensure the learners engaged with the feedback, but this role was reduced as learners matured.

Lottie: In primary school ... I suppose we're teaching them to kind of take in feedback I guess ... So I think like the level of taking responsibility and your independence for learning kind of gradually becomes more and more as the years go by ... so as a teacher I'm doing more than just giving feedback.

Both Lottie and Lilly suggest that, in terms of responding to feedback, learners are central in higher education but that in primary schools, the teachers remain more significant. Rather than necessarily implying a development of roles and responsibilities, this distinction can be attributed to the unique dual roles of the participants. In other words, when they are in the role of learner, they are responsible; when they are the teacher, they are responsible too. The focus on the self may reflect the participants' egocentrism, although this could also reflect the increased responsibilities of university students in comparison to learners in school.

Sapna felt that a more learner-centric view of feedback made the process less emotionally challenging.

Sapna: If you can get them to verbalise, to really look at their work ... then they're more likely to take it on board, they feel some ownership of it and it feels less critical.

The softening of emotional impact is a result of the less hierarchical power dynamic between teacher and learner when roles and responsibilities are shared. Theoretically, a more learner-centric model does not view the judgment of the teacher as the only 'truth'.

Evie indicated that the learner-centric view of feedback was most prized, reflecting the work of others (Sadler, 1989). To Evie, this was because there were knock-on implications in terms of confidence and motivation.

Evie: I think that's … almost like the best … form of feedback that you can get when … if they can come to it on their own then they can feel prouder of it and if you can say well … you did that on your own that's great, you must be really proud of yourself … that almost gives them the confidence.

Evie suggests that it is important that learners (in the school context at least) are able to be autonomous and independent, identifying and acting upon feedback for themselves. This more learner-centric model of feedback links to a number of concepts that can be viewed as part of 'learnacy', generally positioned within the formative assessment discourse. Learnacy (Butler and Winne, 1995) includes meta-learning, or learning about learning, and aims to develop autonomous learners who have ownership of the learning process. Learning is positioned as dynamic and equitable with both learner and teacher learning through shared interaction, experience and dialogue (Evans, 2013). However, given that the feedback models are not age specific, it is hard to see how such a learner-centric view might apply to primary-age children as well as students in higher education. Indeed, does any learner who is part of a teacher–learner relationship really have autonomy and control when the teacher/tutor is professionally responsible for the curriculum, mode of delivery and the judgement about attainment? Is it that expectations of younger learners' capabilities have actually been distorted by the teacher-centric practice that has existed in schools for so long and has arguably been exacerbated or amplified in recent years? Teacher-centricity is valued, distributed and accounted for through policy and practice.

Several participants also commented on learners having a key role in higher education. For example, Daisy stated she had responsibilities as a learner.

Daisy: But then I think it's my responsibility to build on it and to take it into consideration.

As a learner, Daisy implies a degree of learner responsibility and independence. Molloy and Boud (2013) develop this in their higher education model of feedback known as 'Feedback Mark 2'. Here the learner *'actively makes links between their goals in learning, the strategies or approaches they use to achieve this target and their actual performance outcomes'* and as such has *'significant agency and choice'* (2013, p 23). This discourse equates to a more sustainable model of assessment as potentially it leads to more long-term attributes and skills for the autonomous learner.

Reflection

> » As an ITE practitioner, to what extent does your practice link to Feedback Mark 2, a more sustainable view of assessment where autonomous attributes and skills are developed?

Arguably being an autonomous learner will also include having the necessary beliefs to recognise that they can and will achieve. Indeed, some of the participants discussed how feedback influenced the way they thought about themselves and their ability to achieve.

Lottie: Well, originally I thought that like getting feedback was constructive and motivating however after [placement] I feel like it's actually demotivated me hugely … because … the feedback that I got was always 'not improving', I wasn't improving, it just kind of demotivated me … I feel like I did act on the feedback and I was quite positive about it at first but the more I kept trying things and then my feedback would get worse and I was like 'oh my god like what am I doing that's wrong?' and then I was trying everything in my power to be able to change things and it still wasn't getting any better … I just thought 'what's the point of looking at it? Like what is the point?'

Lottie is implying that the lack of affirmatory or positive comments influenced her self-belief. Too many 'deficit' comments, no matter how constructive, negatively influenced her motivation, which ultimately affected her ability or will to engage with the feedback. A negative judgement damaged her *'self-efficacy, or sense of ability to be effective'* (Gibbs and Simpson, 2004, p 11). Self-efficacy is what Sadler describes as the ultimate goal of feedback (1989), but self-belief is not enough in itself; learners also need to regulate their performance if they are to be autonomous. Having said that, if we assume that self-efficacy has strong overlaps with motivation, self-efficacy will be necessary if learners are to self-regulate (Altun and Erden, 2013) and conversely the ability to regulate one's own learning will support the learner's self-efficacy (Zumbrunn, Tadlock and Roberts, 2011). Gaskill and Woolfolk (2002, p 192) describe self-efficacy and self-regulation as a *'dynamic duo'*.

If we return to Lottie, we can see how her self-efficacy was eroded over time when her initial interview is compared to the later one.

Lottie: Even if it [feedback] is bad, it's constructive and you work harder to build on negative feedback … At least for the next time we can work on those and the negative comments are the ones that make us a great teacher.

Lottie: It sounds bad because this is not me at all, it was just like 'what is the point? what is the point in me even trying?'

Wiliam (2011) noted that learners' self-efficacy tended to decrease through schooling and the same appears to be true for Lottie. This raises the question of whether feedback practices on her ITE programme were responsible for this.

Positive feedback could conversely enable student teachers to become more confident in their own abilities.

Lilly: Yeah, as a learner you feed off it almost ... like you need to know if you're doing it right or doing it wrong and you need to have confidence in yourself now and just go with it.

The use of the word *'feed'* is significant. The feedback *feeds* self-efficacy in the *'survival stage'* of teacher development until it is firmly in place by the *'mastery'* stage (Furlong and Maynard, 1995, p 68). Feedback can therefore provide reassurance that current performance is *'incremental rather than fixed'* (Wiliam, 2011, p 119).

Reflection tends to be a key feature of any ITE programme. The ability to self-evaluate, reflect and identify future improvements can be equated to self-regulation as a key element in learnacy. Self-regulation is defined as how learners regulate their own thinking, learning goals, next steps and strategies (Butler and Winne, 1995; Zumbrunn, Tadlock and Roberts, 2011; Nicol and Macfarlane-Dick, 2006; Hattie and Timperley, 2007; Altun and Erden, 2013). Self-regulation places the learner centre stage but also recognises that the learner does not work in isolation: they are *'guided and constrained by their goals and the contextual features of the environment'* (Nicol and Macfarlane-Dick, 2006, p 201). In this way, the teacher has a role as well.

As teachers, student teachers can be keen to develop self-regulatory behaviour in their pupils. Lilly stated that she felt the teacher's role was to guide the children towards independence by supporting *'participation and dialogue'* (Carless and Boud, 2018, p 1316) but was aware of the contradictions of coaching learners towards independence.

Lilly: It's to help encourage children gain the independence and maybe ... have them gain confidence in their own abilities ... To help them see where they've succeeded. It depends on the teacher ... to either guide you to tell you what you have done well because, how do you know ... so giving them the tools in order for them to progress independently as well.

Eraut states, *'we need more feedback on feedback'* (2006, p 118 cited in Evans, 2013, p 72), or we could even say we need more learning about learning (Thoutenhoofd and Pirrie, 2015). Carless et al (2011) agree that learners are rarely taught how to use the feedback they receive. Knowing how to engage with feedback means that learners are more likely to self-regulate, which in turn means they are more likely to give themselves feedback (Nicol and Macfarlane-Dick, 2006).

Reflections

» As an ITE practitioner, do you support student teachers' self-regulation by giving feedback on feedback?

» Do you support student teachers in developing pupil self-regulation?

» If so, how, and how do you know it is having the desired effect?

» Given the focus on meta-cognition in the Core Content Framework (Department for Education, 2019b), how could you ensure feedback on feedback is included within your programme design?

IN A **NUTSHELL**

This chapter has argued that:

- student teachers demonstrate a pedagogical understanding of the value of feedback;

- these understandings often align with the discourses within policy and the standards;

- a teacher-centric view tends to prevail, although student teachers do have a desire, as teachers, to support learner autonomy;

- feedback can influence self-efficacy and self-regulation in both a positive and negative sense.

REFLECTIONS ON **CRITICAL ISSUES**

For student teachers, understandings of feedback often have a pedagogical dimension, and these, understandably, are often aligned to the prevailing discourses in policy. Implied discourses within the Teachers' Standards (DfE, 2012) had further value to particular discourses. These are evident more clearly when student teachers are in the role of teacher. However, as has been found, these are not mutually exclusive, with conceptions often coexisting and sometimes contradicting each other. The conceptions were also sometimes teacher specific, sometimes learner specific and sometimes moved between and across learner and teacher. Conceptions of feedback were therefore fluid, dynamic and open to the influence of the role and context. The discussion raises some interesting questions for the ITE sector where pedagogical understandings of feedback encouraged in the teaching practice of student teachers are not always evident in our practice as tutors within higher education. Given that our own practice is a useful form of modelling, closer alignment between the two is worthy of further investigation.

CHAPTER 4 | RELATIONAL UNDERSTANDINGS OF FEEDBACK

CRITICAL ISSUES

This chapter explores the following critical issues.

- *Is face-to-face feedback necessarily dialogic?*

- *Does feedback have a relational dimension?*

- *Is face-to-face feedback more effective at building relationships?*

- *Is it important to know and be known by the person giving feedback?*

This chapter uses reading and student teacher comments to exemplify an exploration of the relational dimensions of feedback and, in doing so, the discussion complements Esterhazy's assertion that '*feedback is inherently relational … influenced by social structures and discourses that shape the socio-cultural practices of our educational institutions*' (2018, p 1303). This includes how the standards agenda may be influencing the feedback relationship as professionals walk '*the tightrope*' between meeting the requirements of the state and building multiple relationships (Rodgers and Scott, 2008, p 735).

Is face-to-face feedback dialogic?

The term 'dialogic' is frequently used within the literature as a feature of effective feedback (or pedagogy) (Walker, Gleaves and Grey, 2006; Yang and Carless, 2013; Ajjawi and Boud, 2018; Carless and Boud, 2018). It holds currency and value within the discourse and has arguably been transferred from theory to practice in the form of verbal feedback practices. However, verbal feedback is not necessarily dialogic.

Reflections

- » How would you define dialogic?

- » To what extent is it interchangeable with dialogue, verbal or face-to-face feedback?

The term 'dialogic' is often seen as synonymous with face-to-face or verbal feedback. Indeed, these are the terms that student teachers tend to use, rather than dialogic, implying that the form has particular value because it allows for discussion. For example, as a teacher, Sapna implied that dialogue was important if feedback was to lead to progress:

Sapna: ... verbal feedback's immediate. You can question ... you can ask them in a different way so they get [a] chance to respond and let you know... you can better understand what they're saying to you and you can explain in as many different ways as it takes ...

Many student teachers perceived discussion as valuable as it allowed for greater clarity of the feedback message, particularly in comparison to written feedback.

Evie: I would say verbally because I think you can talk it through. You might not understand the written feedback ... you can't interact with it.

However, although these comments argue that verbal feedback is more effective, is the feedback dialogic? The 'talking' it through relates to understanding the 'truth' presented by the feedback giver, rather than collaboratively exploring the message together. Indeed, the language used by several participants to explain the value they attached to face-to-face feedback did not necessarily indicate a dialogic conception of feedback. Words such as 'telling', 'clarity', even 'explaining', in the context it was given, all imply that feedback was a tool for transposing meaning; that is, face-to-face feedback allowed the teacher to transfer *their* meaning to the learner more efficiently. Although Yang and Carless (2013) argue that an emphasis on dialogue is an attempt to move away from a one-way understanding of the feedback process, for the student teachers discussed here, verbal feedback was merely a better vehicle for the transmission of the feedback message.

Evie: I also think feedback is better in person ... I feel like it is easier to understand if somebody is telling you rather than it being written.

Reflections

Reflect upon the verbal feedback you give to the students you work with both in terms of academic work and placement.

» What is the balance of face-to-face versus written?

» Is the face-to-face feedback always dialogic?

» Is it a shared and equal exchange, or is it focused on transposing your message?

Face-to-face feedback that has limited dialogic quality also has a limited relational aspect; the teacher still holds a position of power, passing on knowledge and also passing judgement (Higgins, Hartley and Skelton, 2001). If we consider feedback as a relationship, this is an example of a teacher-centric or '*I-It*' (Buber, 2013) relationship where people are treated as objects instead of full and equitable others, that is, '*treats things, including other people, as objects to be used and experienced—they are means to ends*' (Guilherme and Morgan, 2009, p 566). If the educator is essentially *gifting* feedback to the learner, it is the teacher who holds power and the learner who is passive rather than an equitable other. The ITT framework also supports this view of feedback as a gift by continually stating '*and – following expert input ... receive feedback and improve at*' (Department for Education, 2019b, pp 9–31). The word 'expert' is significant here. Bohm's (2013) analogy of discussion as a game of ping pong is also relevant where ideas (of feedback messages) are batted from player (teacher) to player (learner) until the message is transferred.

Genuine and authentic dialogic talk/learning is underpinned theoretically by dialogism, which is arguably a theoretical aspiration. This conceptualises learning as the co-creation of knowledge through the sharing of understandings through dialogue. Crucially, it results in the emergence of new meaning and also suggests equity between teacher and learner. More often than not, however, the practice described by student teachers links to monologism rather than dialogism as it was based on a single thought discourse (Robinson, 2011). Having said that, the polarisation between dialogism and monologism is perhaps an unhelpful one. There are degrees of equity between teacher and learner and possibly degrees of solo construction/co-construction, and it is perhaps naive to aspire to an equitable relationship given the standards agenda that is such a feature of the English education system.

Some student teachers, however, do express a more dialogic view of feedback.

Sapna: It's about giving the feedback but then taking the time to make sure that the feedback has been understood, and also exactly what the next step should be, and involving the learner in those next steps so that ... you come up with a plan together rather than just going 'right there you go, there's your feedback, crack on', ... it's more dialogic ... it's a cycle ... it's reciprocal.

Sapna's comments represent a more adaptive, discursive and interactive view of feedback, although *'coming up with a plan together'* is again unlikely to be totally equitable given the inherent power dynamics between teacher and learner.

Some of the apparent confusion around dialogic versus verbal feedback and transmission versus co-construction of knowledge may in part be a consequence of the social-cultural influence of neoliberalism on education policy and practices. The relational dimension of feedback is certainly an area that requires nuanced and considered understanding, and often there is no space for this within a performance-focused, compliant, technical and dominant view of teaching and learning (Bailey and Garner, 2010; Yang and Carless, 2013). It is not therefore surprising that terminology and conceptions are used interchangeably by the participants. Walker, Gleaves and Grey go further by suggesting that true dialogic pedagogy is now rare because of the *'confines of a mass education system'* (2006, p 260). The influence of the context is undeniably powerful.

Face-to-face feedback and the teacher–learner relationship

This section considers if feedback is itself a vehicle for developing relationships as well as understanding feedback in relational terms. Buber (2013) suggests that meaningful relationships (I–Thou relationships) are defined by knowing each other as a whole being and, when applied to the educational context, this includes recognising the potential of the learner. The participants studied here did view face-to-face feedback as a means of 'knowing the learner' and recognising 'potential' in that feedback allowed for misconceptions to be revealed and meaning to be clarified.

According to Buber (2013, see also Beck, 1992) true dialogue is key to meaningful relationships as it means treating others appropriately and humanely (Stern, 2007) and knowing them as a *whole* (or at least as much as this is possible within an educational setting). The participants indicated that face-to-face feedback allowed for this; they felt it was individual and personable, certainly in comparison to written feedback.

Evie: Written feedback is less personable.

There is evidence that written feedback presents a reduced opportunity to develop meaningful relationships in that, particularly when anonymous, it depersonalises the interaction, promotes monologism and increases the distance between teacher and learner (Pitt and Winstone, 2018). Given the focus on anonymous written feedback within HE institutions, this is interesting and raises questions about this being the 'quality' practice.

There is potential for verbal dialogic feedback to do the opposite (Carless and Boud, 2018) and, as such, to build relationships. As a teacher, Lilly appeared to value verbal feedback as it allowed her to demonstrate care.

Lilly: Yeah, I think it shows the child that you really care about their work and you're taking an interest in their work and their development.

However, is a caring relationship really fully possible? It may be an ideal, but the transference of the associated values is more problematic. 'Caring for learners' is more than likely to be restricted to caring for them in an academic sense in order that learners can make the necessary progress. Educational relationships are arguably not full caring relationships. Indeed, Walker, Gleaves and Grey (2006) argue that the influence of relationships on learning and teaching is largely ignored and may be responsible for wider issues within higher education, for example, student dropout and resilience. Maybe educators and policymakers still have some way to go in recognising the fuller relationship between educators and learners.

Reflections

» To what extent do you think your feedback with students has relational qualities? Consider:

- academic written feedback;

- academic verbal feedback;

- placement written feedback;

- placement verbal feedback.

» Which of these allow you to build as well as maintain a relationship?

One reason why face-to-face feedback could be considered as better at building or maintaining relationships is that, for the participants referenced here, it is seen as softening the emotional impact on the learner; written feedback was viewed as more likely to produce a strong negative emotional response. This resonates with evidence within the literature, which finds that feedback is capable of evoking negative and/or defensive affective reactions, which have far-reaching consequences (Molloy, Borrell-Carrió and Epstein, 2012; Naismith and Lajoie, 2018; Carless and Boud, 2018). In this context, 'affect' refers to *'feelings, emotions and attitudes'* (Carless and Boud, 2018, p 1317), all of which, Carless and Boud (2018) argue, can be mediated by good relationships between teacher and learner.

Two participants in particular (Nick and Evie) described strong emotional reactions that included burning written feedback, hiding it and the inability to 'let go'. In this way, the content of the feedback can be viewed as a form of disavowed knowledge (Taubman, 2012) in that it was known, but destabilising, so avoided. It is worth saying that such emotional responses were nearly always in relation to what the participants perceived as negative feedback. By negative they meant critical or carrying a lower mark than had been anticipated.

Nick: When I first got given the feedback it was more angry ... Then it went to disheartened, when I got the feedback and I was just like, 'Really, that's what it's come to?'

Nick's comments go on to indicate not just an initial reaction but also a cycle of grieving each time he revisits the experience: *'I'm still offended by that.'* It is difficult to see how such a reaction would not influence learner engagement with feedback other than negatively. Molloy, Borrell-Carrió and Epstein state that *'emotions act not only as a barrier but also a stimulus in the learning process'* (2012, p 50), but there was little evidence in the research referenced here that upsetting feedback was ever anything but a block to engagement.

As time went on, some participants began to draw a link between face-to-face feedback and the softening of subsequent emotional responses. There was a perception that the alternative form of written feedback could feel more traumatic (indeed, Evie used the word *'trauma'* to describe the experience) as there was less opportunity to moderate the impact through further explanation or reassurance.

Evie: [in reference to written feedback as an alternative] So sometimes you could maybe take bit more of a front to it. You mightn't understand that somebody is just trying to help you or it just might come across as more of a criticism than a positive or a 'You could do this to improve.'

Lilly: Whereas if you're face to face with someone, so giving oral feedback, you can then more say, 'Right, don't worry about it, we can help you move forward, it is nothing to be ashamed of if you haven't done very well.'

One participant, who was prone to avoiding uncomfortable written feedback, felt that face-to-face feedback was more effective as she was *unable* to avoid it. The conversation forced her to engage with the feedback. This does not necessarily imply that dialogic feedback was taking place but rather that there were professional and social niceties associated with a conversation between tutor and learner, which forced her to engage at least at some level. In other words, the perceived professional response was to engage with the feedback, even if the natural emotional response was to do something very different because it threatened self-esteem (Hattie, 2009).

Interviewer: What about if you did a lesson … your mentor said, 'Do you want me to give you some feedback?', how would you deal with that? Would you think 'I don't want to hear it', or would you say 'yes' even though it's going to be hard?

Evie: I would definitely say 'yes' because I think it's rude not to …

Interviewer: But inside what would you be saying?

Evie: 'Oh god, no, don't tell me.' Yeah definitely, and I think I'd say … I'd jump in before they said anything and say 'look, I'm really sorry it was not planned well enough, I know that' and hopefully they'd kind of skip over that fact.

As practising teachers, some participants felt that verbal feedback also meant that they would be able to rephrase sensitively and pick up on non-verbal cues. As such, the feedback would be less emotionally challenging to the students. In other words, the manner in which the feedback was given influenced the way it was received (Hattie and Clarke, 2018), and verbal feedback was considered to be more sensitive, reducing the likelihood of a relationship breakdown and defensive affective reactions.

Sapna: So, unless you'd actually given them the verbal feedback … it would seem quite cold, but if you're crouched down next to them in the classroom, if they're looking worried, you might sort of put your hand on their shoulder or smile at them and reassure them while you're saying it, and none of that's coming out in just the words.

The ITT Core Framework seems to acknowledge the need for sensitivities around pupil feelings, stating *'building effective relationships is easier when pupils believe that their feelings will be considered and understood'* (Department for Education, 2019b, p 26). As ITE professionals, we need to contemplate whether we consider learner feelings in our feedback and how this might influence our relationships.

Reflections

» As an ITE professional, you too will have also received unexpected or (perceived) negative feedback from colleagues, senior staff, partners or students. Has this feedback carried an emotional dimension to it?

» Has it been easier to deal with when conveyed verbally? If so, why?

» Analyse the difference between the written and verbal forms and then apply your conclusions to your own delivery of feedback to student teachers.

Over the period of their programme, some student teachers implied that they became better at separating feedback on learning from feedback about self. This may be a little simplistic as feedback never exists in a vacuum and one cannot necessarily remove the self (Eva et al, 2012). In addition, over time student teachers appeared to connect their experiences of receiving impact to how they then go on to give feedback in the classroom.

Nick: I think that translates into how I was approaching feedback ... with pupils ... especially Year 1s [as] they take things really personally. So, it was about helping them understand that I'm not ... judging your ideas I'm judging whether you can put a full stop and a capital letter on the sentence.

In other words, the emotional experience of receiving feedback as a learner makes student teachers reconsider how to give feedback as a teacher. The duality of experience, as both learner and teacher, informs each role.

Student teachers reflect on their own affective understanding and therefore select verbal feedback as the softer and more sensitive form to use. This supports Zimmerman's (2019) assertion that reflecting on our own lived experiences can provide valuable professional insight. For student teachers it appears that their duality of experience gives them a unique insight into the role of the teacher by transferring the values developed as a learner. The overlap of the teacher/learner identity within a teacher education programme is unique and a key reflective opportunity to be exploited.

Nick: I was nervous of how they would receive it because I knew myself I wouldn't want to receive that sort of feedback presented in that way ... So, I just thought ... have a discussion ...

There is also evidence that the existence of a relationship between feedback giver and receiver lessens the potential emotional impact of feedback. In other words, the *'quality of the relationship between the giver and receiver is significant in leading to learning'* (Askew and Lodge, 2000, p 6).

Nick: It was with [name of tutor] so you know, I have found feedback quite difficult at times, [but, the tutor] pretty much tore it apart. I think what he said would have been harsh if it hadn't have been coming from [name of tutor]. ... And I think it made me think about verbal feedback as ... it relies on relationships ... because I've got that positive relationship with [name of tutor] and there is ... a sense there is a mutual respect there. ... It didn't feel like a criticism, it felt like a critique and a development ... a relationship [is] a fundamental thing ... it affects how it's received and it almost gives you that ... ability to fly above.

Phrases such as *'fly above'* imply that the relationship between teacher and student enabled Nick to rise above the potential emotional consequence and see the broader and more powerful feedback message. It may also be that an existing relationship possibly means discussion is naturally dialogic, collaborative and therefore better received.

Reflections

» As an ITE professional, do you find it easier to give constructive feedback to a student you know well or a student you do not? Why?

» When receiving constructive feedback, do you find it easier from a colleague you know well or one you do not? Why?

It appears therefore that face-to-face feedback is a preferred form of feedback (both as a learner and as a teacher) as it allowed for greater sensitivity, explanation and sometimes dialogic conversation. Furthermore, the stronger the relationship between teacher and learner, the more effective the verbal feedback. However, HE and ITE now have the same performativity demands of other sectors of education, which raises the question of how can face-to-face feedback be monitored and recorded? The conflicting demands of performance and pedagogy are further discussed in Chapter 5.

To be known and to know

There is evidence to suggest that student teachers associate effective feedback with the feedback giver knowing the feedback receiver. This can be understood as a form of personalisation where the feedback giver knows what the learner needs as an individual.

Sapna: To my mind effective feedback, you have to know the person that you're feeding back to or about, to know what they're going to respond to.

This is echoed by Buber's I–Thou relationship as it indicates a fuller relationship where one knows thou as a '*whole being*' and is able to '*affirm him in his wholeness*' (Buber, 2013, p 92), and also by Hattie and Clarke who link learning to students being secure in the '*knowledge that the teacher cares about and likes them*' (2018, p 83).

Student teachers appear to feel that being known is a two-way process; many wanted to be known and also know the person giving the feedback, further supporting the mutuality of knowing within the relationship.

Lilly: That's kind of unknown and it's also a scary thing because now it's university ... for instance, at school you knew who was marking it and I felt more comfortable gaining feedback in secondary school compared to now.

There is variation around this conception. Some, but not all, of the participants referenced in this text felt very strongly that they needed to know who was providing the feedback as this would have implications in terms of how it was received. Recognising the educator's potential subsequently affected the value the participants attached to the feedback. Deci and Ryan's (2008) self-determination theory supports this further. This framework for motivation asserts that one (of the three) necessary psychological need for motivation is relatedness: the sense of feeling understood and cared for. Given that there is a correlation between the participants' sense of being known and their willingness to engage with the feedback, Ryan and Deci's (2008) relatedness need was also being met.

Knowing the learner appears less significant in the school setting. The first example below refers to identifying achievement-centred targets personal to the pupil, and the second indicates a broader and more holistic view of meeting a child's individual needs.

Daisy: So it's like giving the feedback that's relevant to that child's target, so not just saying in general like have you met the learning objective … it's like altering that feedback depending on the child.

Sapna: To my mind effective feedback, you have to know the person that you're feeding back to or about, to know what they're going to respond to.

It appears teachers need to know the learner well in order to provide appropriately personalised feedback if the feedback is to have a formative consequence.

Some student teachers support a more learner-centred model of feedback where learners are responsible for identifying and acting upon their own learning goals (Sadler, 1989). This is also reliant on knowing – knowing oneself. Self-efficacy (Sadler, 1989) and self-regulation (Bandura, 1991; Butler and Winne, 1995) both include a reference to knowing one's self (as a learner) in order to make judgements about current understanding/performance and identify a suitable action to close the learning gap. However, statements made by student teachers, such as Sam (below), suggest that learners are not always able to meet such high expectations and still rely on the teacher to identify the next steps.

Sam: I wanted them to tell me that they were doing it wrong instead of me saying you're not writing that sentence properly. I wanted them to be able to put their hand up … so I wanted them to pick it out instead of me. Because I think they have to recognise what they're doing wrong before you can actually move the learning on.

Although being known, and knowing the feedback giver, appears significant, the context of peer feedback adds another interesting dimension. Here, the 'knowing' that exists between peers can be viewed as counterproductive. For example, Sapna implied that feedback was only meaningful if it came from somebody she respected professionally rather than knew personally.

Sapna: … because the only other people before who'd seen me were … friends … or [people I knew] personally. So, when you hear people who like you anyway telling you that you're good, you kind of just go, 'Yeah, yeah, whatever.' But when someone who's only met you a couple of months ago and only seen you for a few days really, sees some potential in you then that's a lot more meaningful.

This is a teacher-centric view of feedback that also presents feedback as a form of validation. In Sapna's case, feedback validated her professional identity, but conversely she also treated peer feedback with an element of mistrust, despite peers knowing her better and arguably more holistically. Knowing a learner as a whole (Buber, 2013) was not always conducive to learning.

Sapna: It's always nice to hear someone say, 'Oh, that's really good', but what are you basing that opinion on? It's not on years of expertise. Are you just being polite, or can you recognise good work when you see it?

Sapna's apparent uncomfortableness in relation to peer feedback was not uncommon amongst student teachers. It appears that the peer-to-peer relationship was not necessarily trustworthy when it came to feedback.

Sam: I'd rather not have peer feedback. I like it just going to a teacher ... if you sat with a friend who's peer 'feedbacking' then it's not going to be genuine.

Interestingly, this may be because student teachers feel too known by their peers. Knowing a peer well made the feedback giver too aware of the possible emotional connotations, and this reduced the value of the feedback, suggesting a tension between being known and being too well known.

Sam: I think that it needs to come from someone you don't know to eliminate the personal response, but I think that I would value someone I know's feedback more than someone I don't know.

The contradictions expressed about peer feedback by some of the participants in some way reflect some of the contradictions in the literature. Carless and Boud argue that peer feedback reduces the likelihood *'of power-differentials and negative emotional reactions'* (2018, p 1312), but Sluijsmans, Brand-Gruwel and van Merriënboer (2002) acknowledge that giving feedback to peers is viewed as difficult, risky and often unfair. Here we see how significant the affective dimensions of feedback are and how these ultimately impact other understandings of feedback. For some student teachers, a degree of heightened emotional sensitivity was compounded by a reduced sense of trust in the feedback giver when the giver was a peer. This was because of mistrust in both the feedback giver's expertise and their intention.

Daisy: You're a tutor I feel like we, sort of, not trust your opinion more but, we understand that you've sort of got more knowledge than our peers. So if a tutor was to give us constructive criticism you would be like 'okay, that's a good plan' – we'll try and implement that. Whereas if our peers said something to us we might think 'oh that's a bit rude' because we're on the same level as peers so it might be a bit more difficult to give negative feedback if you're sort of like equal in a situation ... I think it's [peer feedback] good but then obviously because we're being careful not to be mean it might not be that.

This further reveals a teacher-centric (knowledgeable other) view of feedback, as peers were not considered to be more knowledgeable. In addition, it illustrates some of the complexities within the feedback relationship. Certainly, these participants seem to be describing a personal transaction (MacMurray, 1961, cited in Jarvis, 1995) and an I–Thou relationship where the '*whole being*' is recognised (Buber, 2013). However, the 'wholeness' is focused on personal sensitivities which, rather than enhancing the relationship, ultimately impedes it within the feedback context.

Reflection

» If you have made use of peer feedback in your own teaching, reflect on how this has gone. Consider:

– student engagement and enthusiasm;

– quality of feedback provided;

– your role in the process.

Interestingly, when student teachers discuss peer feedback as a teacher, it is positive. In this context, the participants are unaware of any difficulties of trust and expertise between the paired pupils. One possible explanation may be because peer feedback is a relatively efficient way to provide feedback in the classroom, allowing a teacher to meet the feedback standard without providing feedback themselves. One wonders whether peer feedback is another example of strategized practice, that is, a strategy rather than a principled pedagogical approach. Sam was aware of how the practice of talk partners can both be relatively superficial and potentially effective.

Sam: I used talk partners in school, … I did produce some play script writing and I got the children to work in small groups and give peer feedback to each other and I was expecting … them to write things like 'Oh it is funny. I like your character name' whatever, but they really did think about it … and they really thought about that individual.

The different relationships experienced by the participants do reveal variation within the relational economies, including variation in conceptions of being known.

IN A NUTSHELL

This chapter has argued that:

• feedback can be understood as a relational experience and has relational qualities;

• face-to-face feedback is valued as it is seen to provide clarity and softening potential emotional impact;

• face-to-face feedback assists in the building of relationships although is not always dialogic;

• for both teacher and learner, being known is significant if feedback is to be relatable and engaged with.

REFLECTIONS ON **CRITICAL ISSUES**

As Ajjawi and Boud state, *'feedback is a communicative act and a social process in which power, emotion and discourse impact on how messages are constructed, interpreted and acted upon'* (2018, p 1108), and as such it is difficult to conceptualise feedback without reference to relational aspects. This is perhaps even more the case for student teachers who have to develop, maintain and tolerate multiple relationships in multiple contexts; their experience of multiple relationships undoubtedly influences the very presence of relational economies in their understanding. Indeed Zimmerman states that teacher education should be framed as a *'relational pedagogy'* (2019, p 185) as it is a *'relational experience'* (2019, p 187).

As this chapter has explored, student teachers understand feedback as a key mechanism for building these relationships and, indeed, relationships build the effectiveness of the feedback. Experiencing feedback as a learner appears to have a direct influence on how student teachers seek to give feedback as a teacher; they are sensitive to how it will be received and often choose face-to-face feedback as a result. As teachers, student teachers feel they should know their pupils as people and also know what they need. Conversely, as learners, they are conscious of being too well known and, as a result, have some difficulties with peer feedback even though they find it a useful strategy as a teacher. As with other understandings of feedback, relational aspects are varied, often contradictory, and yet do sometimes transfer across the roles of teacher and learner.

Earlier chapters have considered the relational and pedagogical dimensions of feedback. In a similar way, this chapter now explores the moral aspects of feedback using illustrative comments from student teachers.

Does teaching have a moral dimension?

Sayer (2000) discusses how moral dimensions include the '*norms and sentiments regarding the responsibilities and rights of individuals and institutions with respect to others*' that '*go beyond matters of justice and equality, to conceptions of the good*' (p 1). In other words, moral dimensions deal with values and actions of feedback viewed as being the *right* or *good* thing. Of course, education itself is often seen as inherently moral. Oser (2014) argues that educational decision making has an ethical/moral dimension (2014) and for many teachers, a guiding moral purpose reflects their values, purpose (Pantić and Florian, 2015).

Reflection

» How often are your educational actions associated with doing the *right thing?* Try to avoid actions that are only dictated by policy.

Literature related to both motivation to teach and career satisfaction also reveals a strong correlation between teaching and a moral and ethical purpose. Generally, the literature suggests that there are three main identified motivations: intrinsic, extrinsic and altruistic (Watt et al, 2012; Richardson and Watt, 2006; Heinz, 2015; Friedman, 2016; Salifu and Agbenyega, 2016), with altruistic motivations consistently identified as a strong reason for choosing teaching (Richardson and Watt, 2006). If we use Friedman's (Friedman, 2016, p 630) definition of altruism, '*worrying about or caring for the fate of others, or as a behaviour that offers benefit to others, that involves investment on the part of the bestowing person*', it is possible to position both altruism and teaching per se as moral and ethical callings. The desire to '*make a difference*' or '*impart[ing] wisdom or knowledge*' (Arthur et al, 2015, p 16) appears to be a prerequisite to teaching. Lorite summarises this rather well by stating altruistic views of teaching are '*based on traditional nineteenth century perceptions of teaching as a special mission of moral worth*' (2002, cited in Heinz, 2015, p 267).

Is feedback a gift and, if so, how should we behave when we receive it?

If teaching is positioned as altruistic, it carries with it a connotation that it is somehow a charitable bestowing of knowledge to the learner; feedback is a mechanism for this. Subsequently, although the beneficiary is the learner, the feedback giver is the holder of knowledge and therefore has power. So if helping others might serve to '*feed*' the teacher's '*narcissistic appetite*' (Friedman, 2016, p 631) and indeed fill the lack they feel in terms of the ideal teacher, feedback allows this teacher needs to be met.

Reflections

» From your experience interviewing and working alongside student teachers, does 'making a difference' feature either implicitly or explicitly?

» Do you feel this serves altruistic or narcissistic needs?

Student teacher comments do support the view that tutors and mentors are seen as knowledgeable others.

Evie: [in reference to her tutor and the feedback she gave] She's more knowledgeable than us and knows more about PE and things, so we appreciated that.

The use of the word '*appreciate*' also supports the idea that feedback can be conceived as a gift from a knowledgeable other to the learner and for which the learner should be grateful. If a feedback giver is viewed as comparatively more knowledgeable than the receiver (and to have relevant expertise), there is an implied respect: the feedback is 'right' and should be listened to.

Daisy: You're a tutor I feel like we, sort of, not trust your opinion more but, we understand that you've sort of got more knowledge than our peers. So if a tutor was to give us constructive criticism you would be like, okay, that's a good plan – we'll try and implement that.

Such comments imply a recognition that the learner has the responsibility to take the feedback on, or rather accept, the advice. This seems to be a moral convention; when a learner is offered the gift of knowledge from a respected other, it is only polite, and dutiful, to accept this advice. As Clouder and Adefila (2016) put it, a tacit agreement represents a gift exchange.

Reflections

» As an ITE professional, do you think feedback carries with it a tacit agreement that it should be acted upon?

» Consider when you give both academic and placement feedback to student teachers. How do you expect them to respond to the feedback?

» How do you feel if they don't?

» Is this also true when you are receiving feedback from other professionals?

If we consider student teacher conceptions of feedback when they are in the role of teacher, notions of feedback as a gift appear to be slightly more variable. Generally, student teachers still conceptualise feedback as a gift from themselves (as the teacher) to the learner – they know the next right steps or the missing knowledge.

Daisy: … Because in a teaching situation I am the expert, so I know the correct answer …

However, although in the role of a learner, student teachers consider it to be morally right to respond to this 'gift' from a more knowledgeable other when acting as a teacher, the responsibility to respond is also their (as teachers) moral responsibility.

Daisy: I think, as teachers, we sort of make the children respond to feedback …

Interviewer: [in reference to encouraging children to respond to feedback] So, do you think the kids in year 2 are still relying on you?

Lottie: Yeah, I think they are but they're not at the same time. I suppose … if you correcting their work, … and you have done it green and you are asking them to go through and do the corrections and they don't know what to do then, … I suppose it is my fault, I guess …

Lottie's use of the word '*fault*' indicates blame and doing the 'wrong' thing. Lottie feels the burden of doing what she perceives to be the right thing, both morally and professionally. Other student teachers also imply that teachers had some, but not full, responsibility.

Evie: … So almost not saying to them explicitly 'oh you're getting, you're getting this bit wrong, you need to work on that' and you giving that feedback, it's more the children almost feeding back to you but actually helping themselves, do you know what I mean?

If responding to feedback is a learner's moral duty, in reaction to the gift given by another, learners may need support to understand this. As Arthur (2015) states, '*school teachers play a critical role in the formation of young people, shaping the moral character of their students. The best teachers exemplify a set of virtues which they demonstrate through personal example*' (2015 p 5). Modelling how to respond to feedback is a way of demonstrating the practice to the learners.

Reflections

The English Teachers' Standards state '*give pupils regular feedback ... and encourage pupils to respond to the feedback*' (DfE, 2012, p 12). Consider:

» whether your ITE curriculum covers both of these in equal measure;

» whether your own use of feedback encourages learners to respond;

» whether your own practice models and scaffolds appropriate feedback behaviour.

Does feedback need to be fair?

The student teachers studied frequently mentioned fairness, but this was generally in reference to when the participants were learners. As teachers, there were no references to the need to be fair to the pupils. This in itself is revealing. Within the literature, several personal qualities are attributed to 'good' teaching, but fairness is a common theme. In one particular study, the most frequently identified attribute was fairness (Arthur et al, 2015). Fairness arguably necessitates ethical and moral judgment.

There is evidence in the student teacher comments gathered that experiences of feedback are used to build a picture of how fair a tutor is.

Sapna: When we all got our feedback back, there was almost like a ranking order of the tutors who'd marked and the grades that they gave.

Judgements about a tutor's worth as a giver of feedback are viewed by checking the perceived fairness of the marks/comments given to others. Surveys like the National Student Survey reinforce this, asking whether '*marking and assessment has been fair*' (Ipsos MORI, 2021). Students are encouraged to judge the fairness of the tutors and mentors they work with but what is understood by fairness is open to interpretation.

Reflection

» How do you think your student teachers would define fair feedback? Is it when the mark/judgement reflects:

    – the effort put in?

    – the mark/judgement expected?

    – the mark others receive?

    – the marking and moderation process?

The fact that student teachers are judging the worthiness of feedback based on a perception of fairness is interesting for another reason: it contradicts the teacher-centric feedback as a gift model suggested earlier. Whether or not there is a 'knowledgeable other' is ultimately assigned through the experience of the feedback receiver as it is the feedback receiver who judges what is considered to be the fair 'truth'.

'Doing it for the file': the new morality of accountability

In England, ITE, along with other areas of education, is now tightly controlled by the Standards' agenda, so has this context distorted student teachers' views of what doing the right thing is? Successive education policies over the last 20 years have encouraged the collection of data, which allows for target setting, comparisons, competition and judgement. Furthermore, student teachers have generally been schooled within a system which has prioritised the use of summative data as a performativity tool. They now find themselves not only a product of the system but also part of the system as they navigate the accountability demands of the school policy they experience on placement. Their performance as a student teacher is also measured, evidenced, scrutinised and judged as, in order to achieve Qualified Teacher Status, they need to meet the English Teachers' Standards (DfE, 2012). To complicate matters further, specific standards (DfE, 2012) relate to assessment and feedback, all of which need to be accounted for and evidenced. It is difficult to see how student teachers could not be influenced by the culture that has nurtured them and that they now have to promote in order to be successful.

Reflection

» Think about the route your student teachers take to Qualified Teacher Status (QTS). How often does performance, performativity and accountability influence their experience and understanding? You may want to consider pre-course programme and post programme.

The student teacher data collected suggests that feedback can be conceptualised as a way of evidencing performance. This could be pupils evidencing their learning, or response to feedback, but was more often than not a way of evidencing teacher performance to suit the demands of the school or teacher education system; evidencing progress was the *right thing* to do or at least the *right thing* to demonstrate. This may be because of perceived pedagogical reasons but could also merely indicate compliance or indeed narcissistic needs.

Student teachers appear to conceptualise feedback as evidence for performance largely in the context of written feedback, that is, marking. During the earlier stages of the project used here, written feedback was often the default frame of reference whether the discussion was focused on school or university.

Nick: ... but then I think that some schools are stuck in the mindset of feedback as marking or the feedback that someone wants to see from us is marking ... most staff mean it's about feedback and they're like 'Well, where's your accountability if you don't mark?'

Reflections

> » To what extent do you think evidencing performance has become more important than the performance itself?

> » As an ITE practitioner are your judgements always evidence focused?

> » Do you think this distorts student teacher understanding of what is pedagogically important?

Other student teachers also explicitly state that classroom use of feedback is to provide evidence against the Teachers' Standards (DfE, 2012).

Sam: ... I've got to be able to show that I can respond to it ...

Sam: [in reference to adapting the timings related to the returning of written feedback] ... because I thought they needed it because otherwise I wasn't going to be able to prove the standard [related to pupils acting on feedback].

Similarly, Sam stated that as a learner he valued receiving written feedback as it evidenced his ability to develop. Interestingly, he saw this as evidence for himself rather than an 'other' in that he was the one judging his own performance and progress.

Sam: I think that it's just a sign of progression from the primary school and I suppose it's proof here ...

Interviewer: What do you want the proof for? Proof for what?

Sam: For me to show that I've acted on it, so made it better ...

Interviewer: Who are you proving it to?

Sam: Myself.

The repeated use of the word 'prove' implies an underlying lack of trust between those who are judged and those who are judging. However, if this is the case, Sam distrusts his own judgements. Given that trust is considered key to effective feedback (Carless, 2009; Carless, 2012; Hattie and Clarke, 2018), self-doubt is an interesting consequence of the distrust implicit within the performativity culture (Ball, 2003).

Reflections

> » Although ITE has recently begun to move away from an evidence culture (in response to changing Ofsted policy), do you think that the need to 'prove' progress and performance remains?

> » Is this related to trust, and if so, trust in whom? Do ITE professionals trust student teachers, or do we trust ourselves in providing suitable learning and teaching?

> » Does the need for supporting evidence ultimately reassure us that we have also 'made a difference'?

As student teachers progress towards the award of QTS, some appear to express an increased uneasiness in terms of the conflict between feedback policy and philosophy. This is particularly the case in their role as teacher.

Evie: [in reference to marking] ... I was doing it because I had to do it.

Interviewer: Did [the standards] influence the way you gave feedback or the way you thought about feedback?

Evie: Yes, it probably did. I definitely put those feedback sheets in and perhaps a manuscript of verbal discussions with the child, various bits and pieces but that feels quite forced, almost, you make more of a conscious decision, don't you? ... I was doing it for the file.

Others become aware of the need to be accountable early on and identify elements of feedback practice that are purely for surveillance.

Nick: Well, Ofsted wants to see that we're giving feedback, so we need to use these stamps. I'm just like, 'That's not what they're for!'

As time went on, awareness could increase. Nick became more conscious of the need for him to evidence his feedback practice as a student teacher (who would be judged on his performance) and the tension with what he felt was the purpose of feedback.

Nick: That bit between actually informing children's, by moving someone on and your evidence is like there's an awkward relationship there ... that's the thing I still struggle with and I still think how can my, like ethos of good quality feedback is good quality teaching, fit with a school that then says documented feedback is good for accountability.

Nick's use of other phrases like *'the burden of accountability'*, *'they didn't trust her feedback'* and *'it's like whoever you're interacting with is becoming a customer, and you're not trusted'* all indicate a strength of negative feeling about the implications of accountability as a form of power and control which became stronger over time.

Day (2002) argues that newer teachers are particularly susceptible to feeling the pressures of competency measures as they are likely to be less resistant to changing or challenging policy, more compliant but also more vulnerable. Arguably this is a little more complex, with some student teachers becoming more likely to reflect and critique, albeit with an awareness of the need to be compliant to endure.

Should feedback be honest?

Based on the data collected, when student teachers discuss the need for truth, it is couched in the language of positivity as although honesty is significant, it needs to be handled sensitively to preserve self-esteem and motivation. Balancing sensitivity and constructive honesty reflects what Oser (2014) refers to as the conflict between professional morality and professional standards.

In the context of the classroom, participants had an awareness of tempering honesty in order not to damage self-esteem.

Lottie: Well if you, if you say to a child 'oh this is wrong, this is wrong', you know kind of like diminish any enthusiasm to write. ... And if you approach it in a sensitive way then the child will obviously feel like 'oh well, I didn't get it right but I can improve and I can keep trying and trying and trying.' ... So, it's important to praise them so they don't lose that enthusiasm.

For some participants they were also aware of the need for this within their own learning.

Nick: You're taught to sugar coat things and I think because you get that feedback all through your education then to come to university and just get negative feedback ... is a bit like, well, where is the positive praise because there must have been something good in there as well?

This points to an additional moral dimension associated with honesty. A fundamental purpose of good teaching is arguably to ensure learners are happy and motivated. Deci and Ryan's (2008) model of motivation identifies autonomous motivation (linked to a sense of self) and controlled motivation (which includes some form of external regulation or shaping of behaviours). The links between motivation and feedback that some of the participants describe fall between the two; by using controlled motivation to regulate external behaviour (the feedback), some participants perceived that learners would have a better sense of self and would therefore be more autonomously motivated. However, others suggested that the effect of honest feedback on motivation was very much down to the individual.

Sapna: It's a personality thing because some children you could say 'ah, come on you can do better than this', ... then others you had to really ... boost up the praise first ... then it was a case of sort of having to gently just say right ... So, you had to do all the positive stuff first and then a bit more at the end and the good old positive negative positive sandwich.

This was also the case when participants spoke about their own experiences of honest feedback as a learner; an unbalanced focus on the 'feedback gap' had a negative impact on motivation and self-esteem.

Lottie: I was quite positive about it at first but the more I kept trying things and then my feedback would get worse and I was like 'oh my god, like what am I doing that's wrong?' and then I was trying everything in my power to be able to change things and it still wasn't getting any better ... I just cried all the time. I just thought what's the point of looking at it? Like what is the point? Like I was a bright eyed and bushy tailed student on day 1 in placement and ... towards the end, it was just like 'what is the point? What is the point in me even trying?'

Lottie felt acutely that feedback had been demotivating and implied that this related to her sense of self and was therefore a form of autonomous demotivation. The focus on areas of development, although honest, meant that she had less determination and wanted to give up. Arguably this can be true for all learners. Feedback can therefore impede what could be viewed as an innate need for competence within motivation (Schüler, Sheldon and Fröhlich, 2010).

However, other student teachers indicate that if constructive feedback was smothered with too much praise, it can also be demotivating.

Daisy: ... if you got praised for every single thing that you did right every day then you'd be there forever, because if you get praised all the time ... it's not really effective. So, that might be a bit demotivating as well.

This is supported by Murtagh (2014) who found that although teachers often focus on trying to make their feedback motivating, sometimes the opposite occurs as learners become overdependent on the teacher, thereby reducing autonomous motivation. Also, praise tends to be formed as evaluative rather than constructive feedback. This may feel sensitive but can result in '*devaluing the evaluation to the point where its function was merely phatic*' (Alexander, 2000, cited in Murtagh, 2014, p 519); feedback serves to create goodwill and good feeling rather than move the learning forward.

The link between sensitive feedback and motivation is a conception where student teachers often translate their own experiences as a learner to the way they give feedback as a teacher. In other words, student teachers have a strong moral purpose in ensuring their pupils do not feel the same way that they themselves have felt when they experience what is perceived to be insensitive feedback.

Daisy: I've sort of believed that [the necessity for positive feedback] more strongly ... last year when I was on placement my mentor didn't do the positive thing, she just essentially was very negative for about an hour and then told me what was good, which was a bit depressing, really. So that made me think that's not what I need to do.

The need, or not, to tell the truth within feedback certainly has a moral dimension and student teachers are aware (and sometimes feel the burden) of the implications of truth to motivation.

Becoming a *'good'* teacher?

Student teachers will have their identity significantly influenced by the teachers they encounter (Buchanan, 2015), and this will include differing moral compasses which may present themselves in feedback practice.

They could begin training with an expectation that *good* teachers would behave in a certain way and hold certain moral values and, as novices, pursue this ideal. Indeed, *'early idealism'* (Furlong and Maynard, 1995 p 73) has certainly been recognised as a stage of teacher development, which is formed from expectations and experience of significant teachers in a student teacher's past. However, the process of becoming a teacher will challenge student teacher ideals of what a good teacher is as they encounter other class teachers, mentors and tutors, as well as respond to the symbolic ideals presented in policy and discourse.

Reflections

» Who decides whether a teacher is good? The teacher? The mentor? The tutor? The pupils?

» What does *good* mean? Is the definition solely based on grading criteria or standards?

Feedback can either reinforce or challenge student teacher identity. In the study referenced here, Sapna discussed how positive feedback from her mentor had authenticated the belief that she could be a good teacher. This was particularly meaningful as it came from somebody she respected as a *'good'* teacher and Sapna therefore really valued her opinion.

Sapna: People have said for years, 'You should teach', friends who are teachers, family members and I've always kind of gone, 'But what if I'm not very good?' ... So for someone who's seen me interacting, who isn't closely related [to me] ... when someone who's only met you a couple of months ago ... sees some potential in you then that's a lot more meaningful ... I think your first response is, 'Really?! You think that? Okay', and then you start to think, 'Well, maybe I am. Maybe I can.'

Conversely, other participants discussed how feedback had felt like an assault on their identity. It is difficult to tell whether this diminished or reinforced their identity, but it certainly unsettled them by causing a questioning of their values and self-perception. Nick referred to the fact that the feedback appeared to criticise something in which he felt there was a degree of competence (in this case, creativity).

Nick: ... you're sort of putting yourself out there a little bit ... you feel more vulnerable ... but that's what I know I can do well ... because you care about it so much it does feel a lot more personal.

This indicates that feedback was viewed as exposing, particularly in relation to his personal identity and perception of competence.

Reflections

» How has feedback reinforced or challenged your own professional identity as a teacher educator?

» Can you think of a time when the feedback you have provided has affected a student teacher either positively or negatively? Try to analyse why this was.

Arguably notions of identity could be linked to performance standards or any measure that attempts to quantify what a good teacher is. As Salifu and Agbenyega state, *'teacher identity is constantly being embedded in power relations, ideology, and culture'* (2016, p 62). Buchanan goes further to suggest that the focus on standards and performance, in fact, creates a post-professional rather than a professional model of teaching (Buchanan, 2015) and this will, in turn, encourage a post-professional teacher identity. Maxwell and Schwimmer (2016) suggest that individual teacher identities are often part of a collective norm. For student teachers these norms will include those expressed within their teacher education programme and the norms encountered within their differing school experiences. Identities (whether collective or individual) are practised (Cochran-Smith, 2003); therefore, student teacher identities are likely to be shaped by the feedback practices they encounter (as practising teachers) during school placement.

If teacher identity is formed through experience, for student teachers, this will include their experiences as both a learner and a teacher. This will include observing and engaging with differing feedback practices in the settings in which they are learners and the settings in which they practise feedback themselves. The development of teacher identity by working with other teachers is a form of apprenticeship (Buchanan, 2015), but that is not to say that the values associated with feedback experienced are taken on wholesale.

Evie: [in reference to providing feedback] I mean it is a great way to boost self-esteem ... I think they felt quite proud when I said oh I loved how you've done that there and quite specifically praised them. And then it helps the others kind of boost their kind of work as well ... it's how Mr [mentor's name] feeds back to me and he always starts with a positive and ... it's always constructive criticism and I hope that I use that as well in my teaching when I am giving feedback ... that same kind of structure.

The feedback practice observed and experienced by Evie allowed her identity to be shaped by *'current circumstances'* as it *'is constantly in motion, developing as teachers engage in their daily practices and reflect on their work'* (Buchanan, 2015, p 703). Rodgers and Scott support this, stating that teacher identities are constructed and reconstructed through *'interaction with cultural contexts, institutions, and people with which the self lives, learns, and functions'* (2008, p 751); the potential interactions within a teacher education programme are effectively the conduit for the transfer of feedback practices.

There were also examples of feedback practice that was in opposition to the student teacher's identity.

Daisy: I think in year one you're just a bit blindly following what the school do ... but I think even though I might've been following what the school wanted me to do it wasn't necessarily my opinion ... now I was thinking well ... this isn't the method I'd use or this is the method I'd use for my own class.

Daisy was also able to reflect on how her desired practice had changed over time as her identity became clearer and stronger. This caused some tension when she attempted to negotiate school/national policy and what she felt was important. There is an indication here that feedback practice needed on a school placement may not be based upon what a student teacher views as the *right* action but one that is recognised as necessary to comply with. Given the power dynamics within a final placement, student teacher dilemmas like this can be an unspoken form of *'fearless speech'* (Foucault, 2001). Both Friesen and Besley (2013) and Buchanan (2015) agree that student teachers are frequently faced with struggles such as these as they are simultaneously exposed to differing practice and values, have preconceived identities challenged and become more determined in what they believe makes a good teacher. As Buchanan states, *'the tensions of identity formation during teacher education can be jarring, and aren't always examined explicitly through participation in the program'* (2015, p 703). This is an area worthy of serious consideration by teacher educators.

IN A **NUTSHELL**

This chapter has argued that:

*   teaching and therefore feedback has an inherent moral dimension;

*   student teachers experience the morality of feedback as both learners and teachers; sometimes one influences the other;

*   the drive towards evidence, accountability and the standards agenda has encouraged a new morality;

*   student teachers experience dilemmas associated with what is understood as the *right* thing to do in terms of feedback.

REFLECTIONS ON **CRITICAL ISSUES**

By making reference to both literature and student teacher comments, this chapter has argued that feedback carries particular moral implications. These are experienced by student teachers (as both learners and teachers), and these experiences shape student understanding about what is the *right* thing to do as a teacher. Becoming a student teacher involves exposure to different understandings of the *right* thing; performance measures, policy and the philosophies and approaches of the individuals they work with will all influence student teacher beliefs about what they stand for and how they should behave. Feedback is a mechanism for both reinforcing these beliefs and also highlighting tensions to resolve.

CRITICAL **ISSUES**

This chapter explores the following critical issues.

- *how feedback in ITE can be conceptualised as a model;*

- *the relationship between learner and practising teacher;*

- *the implications for feedback practice moving forward in ITE;*

- *further implications for school practice and higher education.*

Summarising discussions to this point

As we start to consider implications for the future, it is worth recapping the discussions so far. So what have we learnt? Well, first that student teachers straddle higher education, school-age education and of course ITE. All of these have conceptions, policies and practices associated with feedback, some of which are aligned and some that are contradictory. Furthermore, student teachers experience feedback as learners receiving feedback from mentors and tutors and also as practising teachers when they give feedback to the pupils in the classroom. These experiences help to inform student teachers' understandings of feedback in three ways: pedagogical understanding, relational understanding and moral understanding. Through exploring student teacher comments, it has been possible to see how these understandings can coexist and also how they are informed by our own – as ITE practitioners – policies and practices associated with feedback as well as the sociopolitical context ITE operates within. All of these explorations lead to the point of presenting a new conceptual model of feedback for ITE before considering what this means moving forward.

The feedback ribbon: a conceptual model

Existing conceptual models of feedback do not focus on student teachers and often present a rather one-dimensional view of feedback, for example, looking at the pedagogical processes of feedback. As this text has argued, an understanding of feedback does not only have a pedagogical dimension but also have moral and relational aspects. Because of this, the following model is suggested as a way of conceptualising feedback for student teachers.

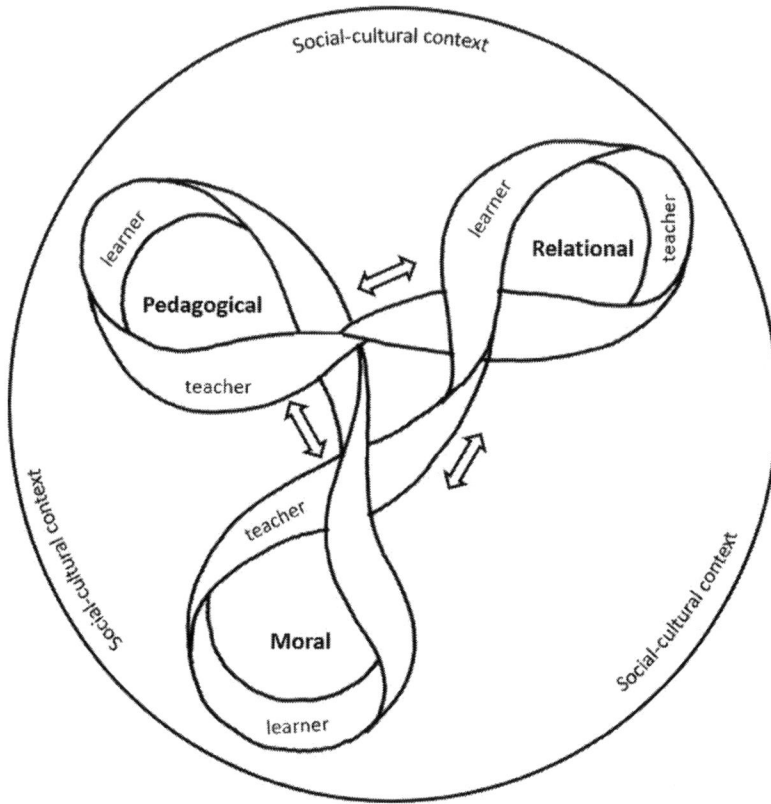

Figure 6.1 The feedback ribbon

The feedback ribbon attempts to demonstrate that developing an understanding of feedback for a student teacher is fluid, dynamic and complex. At its heart, the model posits that feedback can be understood in many different ways, with no one conception necessarily more prized than another. The ribbon of the model signifies the dual experiences of teacher and learner, one on each side. Using a mobius strip, where one side flows into the other in a never-ending manner, the model suggests that for both teacher and learner roles and the experiences that support these, there is an ongoing fluidity and influence between them. Neither role is necessarily more significant than the other; both coexist. The different experiences of teacher and learner inform the student teacher in developing interrelated pedagogical, relational or moral conceptions about feedback. These conceptions are dynamic and are open to change as new experiences present themselves. Furthermore, conceptions are altered further by the unavoidable influence of the social–cultural context (whether its discourses are accepted or resisted). Fairclough's (1992) broad understanding of social–cultural is used here, that is, *'local or global, micro or macro'* (p 286). In other words, within the model, sociocultural includes political policy, national and local specific influences, all of which are significant in ITE.

The model provides a visual representation of the interconnectedness of the pedagogical, relational and moral dimensions of feedback, with one often influencing another, even if for a short period of time; for example, one conception could have consequences for another and vice versa. Although the economies are grouped into separate areas, the model also acknowledges fluidity between them as each cannot be viewed in total isolation. For example, if one understands feedback as corrective and transmissive, the relationships between teacher and learner will be viewed in this way, and there will also be a change to the moral purpose of teaching. Notwithstanding the argument that some of these conceptions can be longstanding, and based on previous experiences as a learner, the model posits that, for student teachers, development is dynamic, not fixed, and open to influence from new experiences and discourses. This is an ever-changing and sometimes messy picture. The fluidity and dynamism of the model is because of the unique role student teachers hold at this time in their careers. Navigating several identities and relationships at once (some with inherent power dynamics) results in a corresponding openness to new conceptions and experiences. In other words, uncertainty in identity encourages openness to suggestion, particularly when some of these suggested conceptions carry the added weight of the standards agenda. It may be that over time, as identity becomes more assured, the fluidity of the model reduces, becoming fixed on particular conceptions.

Reflection

»   To what extent do you feel this model represents:

  −   student teachers' understanding of feedback discussed in this book?

  −   the student teachers with whom you work?

Relationships between the two roles of student and teacher

As has already been outlined, this book has argued that student teachers occupy two different roles as learner and teacher. But how do these two influence one another in terms of feedback as there are further implications from this?

Learner to teacher

It appears that experiences as a learner can directly inform conceptions of feedback as a teacher. The participants referred to within this book found the interview process itself useful in making these connections and encouraging a deeper degree of self-reflection. The dualism of the experiences of teacher and learner, and the associated conceptions, were particularly pertinent to the student teachers, who clearly saw themselves in both roles and had a degree of flexibility in their teacher identity given the stage of their career. One wonders whether, as the student teachers become more assured in their professional teacher identity and begin to view themselves as '*experts*' rather than '*novices*' (Brody and Hadar, 2015), and also cease to be learners in a formal, institutional sense, they may subsequently lose their awareness of their learner identity and hence be less open to listening to this learner voice.

One particular link from learner to teacher was the emotional impact of feedback. As learners, the participants' awareness of how distressing feedback could be, informed their sensitivity around giving feedback as a teacher and verbal feedback was employed as a way of softening this potential harm. Verbal feedback was also more valued as the participants recognised the pedagogical worth of discussing feedback in that it allowed for meaning to be communicated, constructed or co-constructed in greater depth.

Reflection

» Have your own reactions to feedback received (for example, from a peer-reviewed paper) ever informed how you give feedback? For example, have you become more or less sensitive about the language you use? Or do you see the receiving and giving of feedback as totally disconnected experiences?

Although Brown (2011) argues that teachers' conceptions are developed through their own experiences as a learner, in relation to the feedback cycle and the responsibility to complete it, student teachers appear to have a somewhat schizophrenic understanding of feedback. For the student teachers referred to within this book, the *teacher* understanding did not always reflect that of the *learner*. For example, when in the role of teacher, student teachers felt they were responsible for ensuring pupils responded, but when in the role of learner, it was not the tutor's but their own responsibility again. Having said this, of course, student teachers are learners at the same time they are teachers; they are learning about feedback and learning through their experiences of feedback. In reality, the teacher/learner roles overlap.

Teacher to learner

As would probably be expected, over the period of their programme, student teachers appeared to alter their understanding of feedback as they became more aware of the professional duties and responsibilities of feedback related to teaching and learning to be a teacher. As teachers, feedback is understood not solely as a way to promote learning but a useful form of evidence in relation to the participant's ability to meet the Teachers' Standards (DfE, 2012). As has been evidenced in earlier chapters, some student teachers can find it motivating to meet and evidence the expectations of the

Teachers' Standards. Other student teachers appear to retain a more critical approach to meeting these expectations, whilst still recognising that they needed to comply with them. Arguably the presence of any standards that need to be complied with could distort teacher development; in order to comply, development is accelerated but not necessarily robust as change is not based on the development of beliefs but rather practice that will be monitored. As student teachers move through their programmes, they appear, based on the data discussed within this text, to become more self-regulatory in relation to feedback, but, again, this may be related to self-surveillance and compliance rather than autonomy. Having said that, the fact remains that in order to qualify, English teachers need to comply with the Teachers' Standards; self-policing enables them to ultimately be successful, but at what cost? Surely we want teachers who are critical, analytical and reflective rather than merely compliant. Indeed the 2020 Core Content Framework (Department for Education, 2019b) illustrates the inherent contradiction dictating what student teachers need to learn and do but at the same time encouraging critical engagement and reflection (for pupils as well as student teachers).

Reflection

» As an ITE practitioner do you also feel this contradiction? Is it possible to both dictate and comply with centralised expectations in relation to feedback but also develop critical, reflective and autonomous individuals?

Returning to the dual role of student teachers, peer feedback is an area where understanding as a teacher appeared to shape understanding as a learner. Many participants referenced in this text only realised the potential of peer feedback as their programme progressed. This was often because they made use of this approach in the classroom as a teacher, viewed it as valuable (because it was often a key feature of the school discourse in both policy and practice) and therefore started to reconsider their own understanding and conceptions of it as a learner. Some participants had expressed a degree of discomfort when working with peers as learners, particularly earlier in the project. However, realising the value of feedback as practising teachers in schools encouraged the participants to revaluate their own views of peer feedback as learners and often came to understand that peer feedback did have value and hence was worth engaging with. This, therefore, suggests there is potential in explicitly reflecting upon related experiences as a teacher and learner, as one can inform the other.

The duality of the experience of being both a learner and a teacher within a teacher education programme allows for transfer between understandings of feedback to a greater or lesser extent. As such, roles, identities and experiences influence understanding, hence the presence of learner and teacher within the conceptual model (Figure 6.1). The inherent duality in being a student teacher makes their position and their potential for understanding unique and a valuable learning opportunity.

Implications for practice

In the following section, the suggested implications are outlined, beginning with ITE but then moving on to the other related contexts of higher education and school education.

Initial teacher education

Opportunities for low stake discussion and exploration

This book has used interviews from student teachers over a three-year period to explore experiences and understandings of feedback as both learners and practising teachers. It is clear from these interviews that the participants benefitted from having explicit opportunities to discuss, reflect upon and debate complex concepts. These interviews were confidential and separate from any assessments or grading as part of their programme. The low-stakes nature of the interviews assisted an open and honest discussion where participants were able to explore challenging ideas, admit confusions or areas of poor practice. This kind of exploratory discussion arguably allows for connections to be made and trickier, or threshold, concepts to be crossed.

The term 'threshold concepts' was first coined by Meyer and Land to describe concepts that are '*central to achieving mastery of a subject*' (Neve, Wearn and Collett, 2016, p 851). Not only are they deemed to be central, threshold concepts are arguably actually pivotal and critical for developed disciplinary knowledge (Timmerman et al, 2013; Gosselin et al, 2016). Meyer and Land (2005, p 1) describe threshold concepts as '*portals*', which open up '*new ways of thinking*' significant to future learning. Without these, learning will stagnate and will not reach the necessary depth or mastery and the learner cannot fully progress (Nicola-Richmond et al, 2018). A feature of threshold concepts is that they often include a degree of '*troublesome knowledge*' (Perkins, 1999); for example, they can be somewhat counterintuitive, be uncomfortable or go against common sense (Cousin, 2006). Given the individual nature of threshold concepts, they will not necessarily appear in course documentation as a key learning or assessed outcome; they could be related to identity and self. Confronting the potential gulf between student teachers' ideals and the reality of who they are as a teacher, what teaching is and the career they have signed up to will undoubtedly result in an '*identity shift ... entail[ing] troublesome, unsafe journeys*' (Cousin, 2006, p 1).

Tutors could potentially remain largely unaware of the concepts that are blocking the development of further understanding the troublesome nature of the concept. Conventional discussions as part of placement experiences with a mentor or module experiences with a tutor are not necessarily conducive to the open exploration that is necessary, given that mentors and tutors are also responsible for grading student teachers and are in a position of power no matter how approachable we might see ourselves as. With this in mind, one key recommendation or implication for future ITE practice is to build into programme design opportunities for student teachers to discuss and explore key experiences and understandings in a low-stakes context. This does not necessarily need to be with a tutor but, if so, could be a tutor who has a degree of separation from the assessment aspects of the programme.

Experiences as a learner

The book also suggests that conceptions of feedback are often informed through experiences as a learner. There were many examples of how experiences as a learner informed the way that feedback was given as a teacher, for example, a heightened awareness of the need to be sensitive to emotional reactions. An implication for ITE is, therefore, that learner experiences should be explicitly presented to student teachers as a vehicle for encouraging them to face, reflect upon and critique these pre-course and subsequent developing conceptions. More often than not, ITE programmes encourage student teachers to reflect on their experiences as a teacher, although I would suggest that experiences as a learner and how they inform the role of teacher are also very powerful across all aspects, but particularly in relation to feedback. Opportunities to reflect on pre-course experiences in relation to feedback, as well as ongoing experiences of receiving feedback, are all worthy prompts for further analysis and, given that this is a unique period of duality in a teacher's development, should be used before the experiences become more distant.

As ITE practitioners, we need to recognise that student teachers are never novices when it comes to teaching, learning, assessment and feedback. As products of the education system themselves, student teachers join ITE programmes with pre-service beliefs that are significant in shaping understanding (Löfström and Poom-Valickis, 2013; Ní Chróinín and O'Sullivan, 2014; Lee and Schallert, 2016). These learner-situated beliefs could potentially remain (Korthagen, 2004) if not acknowledged or challenged. Indeed, Carless argues that students' preferences (and indeed conceptions) of feedback are often derived from their previous experience where they have developed '*limited absolutist beliefs about knowledge*' (Carless and Boud, 2018, p 1316), supporting Lortie's (1975) ideas around '*apprenticeship of observation*'. If, as Brody and Hadar (2015) suggest, an expert differs from a novice because of an '*intuitive grasp of situations based on a deep tacit understanding*' (p 248), then who is to say that the tacit understanding cannot be developed through experiencing feedback through the role of learner rather than teacher? An expert in feedback is not necessarily an experienced teacher but a learner. As Lee and Schallert (2016) state, '*teachers tend not to put into practice what they were told to do during their ITE but rather what they actually experienced themselves as students*' (p 181). It is vitally important then that their experiences as learners within ITE reflect what we would hope they would do as practising teachers; '*the experience of ... assessment [and feedback] becomes doubly important*' (Lee and Schallert, 2016, p 182).

The Teachers' Standards

It was interesting to note how the language of the Teachers' Standards (DfE, 2012) became part of the educational discourse communicated by the participants over time. This was rarely done critically; the language of the Standards (DfE, 2012) was interpreted as good practice, informed professional identity and was therefore given value. Largely, this was with reference to the participants' conceptions as teachers, implying a degree of buy-in to the standards discourse within the role of teacher (but not necessarily in their role as learners). A further recommendation, therefore, is that ITE programmes should include more critical debate of any standards discourse, particularly in relation to assessment and feedback, and encourage reflective and reflexive links between the statements in the Standards and student teachers' experiences as both a teacher and a learner. This should include a reasoned debate about some of the value-laden terminology and associated practice contained in the Standards. This is not to say the Standards (DfE, 2012) should be dismissed but that they should be engaged with and understood on a more critical, deep and reasoned level. Only by doing so can ITE providers play a greater part in developing transformative future professionals rather than merely promoting compliant technicians (Clarke and Phelan, 2017). Teacher education practitioners should exploit this unique time in student teacher development by encouraging experiences, conceptions and the teacher development narrative to be viewed from both of these perspectives. After all, a teaching career will hopefully extend well beyond the lifetime of any current Teachers' Standards and associated policies and practice.

At the time of writing, ITE practitioners in England are dealing with not only the Standards (DfE, 2012) but also a new Ofsted Framework (Ofsted, 2020), the Core Content Framework (Department for Education, 2019b) and Early Career Framework (Department for Education, 2019a). Despite the reference to critical engagement with research and ongoing reflection within these, it does seem that a particular view of teaching, learning and teacher education is being dictated and ultimately monitored and measured. January 2021 has also seen the announcement of a DfE review of the ITE market and the establishment of a UK Institute for Teaching (Department for Education, 2021). All of these seem to imply a particular view of teaching, learning, curricula, assessment and, of course, feedback. Given that these substantial and significant changes have either been introduced or announced during the COVID pandemic, there is reasonable concern in the sector (Universities' Council for the Education of Teachers, 2020, 2021) about workload, identity and the future of the area. It seems more important than ever that feedback policy in relation to these changes is critically understood rather than simply transferred to programme content.

Higher education

Given that ITE more often than not straddles higher education, it is pertinent to explore the implications for this sector too.

Use of metrics including the National Student Survey

As was outlined in Chapter 2, National Student Survey (NSS) data (Ipsos MORI, 2021) within higher education is viewed as a powerful metric in relation to the quality of feedback. However, arguably this survey has become a distraction to the feedback debate becoming more about quality assurance than the quality of feedback experiences; although these may appear to be the same thing, they are not. A recommendation, therefore, is that policymakers and practitioners should reframe the discourse away from processes related to compliance with university systems and re-examine how feedback is conceptualised and experienced by the students. Becoming focused on procedural aspects has led to '*a prescriptive approach which inhibits learning ... leads students away from the most important aspect of what they should be doing – critical engagement with complex knowledge*' (McArthur, 2018, p 46). Similarly, the new outcomes judgement for HE, the Teaching Excellence Framework (TEF), '*measures everything but excellence in teaching*' (Benn, 2018, p 95). Many 'quality' processes run the risk of stripping out all the possible quality in teaching, assessment and feedback and should not be used to judge effectiveness. Indeed, the quality of feedback should be informed by the experience of the receiver of feedback, as it is only this person who is able to comment on the impact of the feedback. Simply surveying students in relation to four quite narrow questions does not do this adequately enough as, as this book and Wisniewski et al (2020) argue, feedback is much more complex than previously thought.

The relational dimension

A further recommendation is that feedback should be framed as a relationship between the giver and receiver. Practices such as anonymous marking should be re-examined to see how it influences the development, or not, of a relationship. Indeed Pitt (2018) argues that far from increasing perceptions of fairness, such practices ultimately reduce views of fairness because of the negative influence they have on the feedback relationship. A more critical discussion of the far-reaching consequence of feedback practice, beyond compliance with the 'quality' agenda, is necessary within the sector. The importance of the relationship between teacher/tutor and learner was significant in the value and engagement participants attributed to feedback. An implication is that higher education provision should redirect funding from efficiency processes to fund time for feedback relationship building. Investment should allow for learners to meet with tutors or peers and engage with feedback in a personal and dialogic manner. Arguably such a mechanism exists within the well-being services offered at universities but, as has been argued, it is difficult to compartmentalise the relational and the pedagogical. Opportunities for tutors and students to meet on an individual basis to discuss feedback, clarify meaning and minimise emotional consequences would likely increase the value of feedback as it will be better understood and engaged with.

School education

Finally, as ITE students are practising teachers, there are undoubtedly implications for feedback practice in the school sector that have emerged from these discussions.

School feedback practice

As has been outlined in earlier chapters, there is evidence that feedback in schools is sometimes strategized into a series of '*gimmicks*' (Ward, 2008). For example, participants discussed approved formulaic techniques such as: 'green for growth and tickled pink' marking policies, the 'feedback sandwich' approach to giving feedback messages or the use of verbal feedback stamps. These practices were usually enforced at a school level, so student teachers needed to engage fully with them to adhere to school policy. Based on the evidence provided by student teachers, such techniques sometimes presented a rather superficial and mechanistic approach to feedback, without a corresponding critical understanding of the underlying principles, consequences and conceptions of feedback.

The study therefore suggests that in schools, for well-intentioned reasons, the mechanics of feedback have sometimes taken over from the principles and purposes of feedback. The study proposes that such a technical approach to feedback is a consequence of performativity, where teachers need to be seen to do 'more feedback' or a particular school approach to feedback, leaving little time to really examine what good feedback is. Indeed, this is supported by the Department for Education (2016, p 6), who acknowledge that feedback has become a measure of 'teacher performance' (Department for Education, 2016, p 6) rather than necessarily teacher or indeed learner effectiveness. Against this background, Boyle and Charles (2010) argue that formative assessment has been reduced to a 'shopping list of things to do which teachers are trained to operationalise' (p 287), and this study finds this is also true for feedback.

As such, this study asserts that schools should try to develop as sites for critical debate about what feedback is, what is experienced and understood about feedback and what the implications are for the classroom. However, schools do not exist in vacuums and any change away from the 'quick fix' approach to educational development must be supported by those who measure and judge the effectiveness of the school, for example, in England, Ofsted. It is only if the performativity shackles are released from schools that they will have time and confidence to critically examine key areas of pedagogy. This means risk-taking, which is not encouraged in a high-stakes testing culture. However, there have been some hopeful changes more recently. Speaking in reference to the latest school Ofsted Framework (Ofsted, 2019), Amanda Spielman (Chief Inspector) commented that 'inspection may well have unintentionally contributed to the shift by reinforcing the focus on measures. Measures only ever provide a partial picture: inspection should complement, not duplicate, that picture' (Spielman, 2018, p 4). The extent to which 20 years' worth of performative focused educational practice can be let go of remains to be seen, but schools appear to be moving away from feedback being synonymous with marking, with many taking a 'no-marking' approach (Sealy, 2018).

A related implication of the study is that schools should actively discourage any dichotomous discourse where school policy and practice are positioned as either 'good' or 'bad'. Strategies are often actioned because they are now valued as 'good' practice and in direct opposition to what came before. ITE buys into this, too, by taking account of current school policy in programme content and encouraging students to adhere to these practices on placement. This increases the speed of change by encouraging a rather knee-jerk response and sometimes a reductive view of pedagogy. Schools should evaluate any change carefully and accept that feedback is not black and white but complexly grey, with lots of coexisting conceptions that have differing merits; ITE needs to adopt the same approach. Changes to school practice should ideally be research-informed and very carefully evaluated, whilst recognising the difficulties inherent in some of these suggestions in the current high-stakes policy climate.

Verbal feedback

The last suggestion relates to verbal feedback. This was identified as a positive form of feedback for the participants, but the practice did not necessarily reflect truly dialogic principles, meaning potential was not always realised. As a result, it is suggested that schools re-examine what they take to be dialogic practice in light of the theoretical principles of dialogic teaching/dialogism and the research findings in this area. This debate should go beyond the pedagogical objectives of a dialogic approach but also consider the relational and emotional consequences of discussing feedback, for example, the potential for discussion to bring closure to emotionally challenging feedback experiences. Furthermore, schools could also continue to/extend their use of peer feedback with carefully modelled and scaffolded training for the pupils regarding how to give and receive effective feedback to/from a peer. If this was done across primary and secondary schools, an implication may be that some of the more negative conceptions around peer feedback evidenced by the early interviews with the participants could be avoided altogether.

As Schmulian and Coetzee (2019) argue, feedback is significant in any competency-based education and none more so than teacher education. Not only is this because ITE prepares student teachers for classrooms that will hopefully be rich in effective feedback opportunities but also because ITE students are exposed to differing contexts and concepts of feedback. The closer these are either aligned or critically explored, the better it will be for the student teacher.

Reflections

As an ITE practitioner:

» how does the current school feedback policy and practice influence your programme content? Is there alignment or contradiction between programme theoretical content and school practice?

» how does higher education feedback policy and practice compare? Is there alignment or contradiction between programme theoretical content and HE practice?

» how can you square the circle to ensure understandings and experiences of feedback ultimately help student teachers develop a nuanced and deep understanding of feedback, which leads to better classroom practice?

IN A **NUTSHELL**

This chapter has argued that:

- student teachers' understandings of feedback and the way in which these understandings develop require a new conceptual model, the 'feedback ribbon';

- the model allows for differing understandings to coexist, which have relational, moral and pedagogical dimensions representing a more complex understanding of feedback;

- the dual roles that student teachers occupy as both learners and practising teachers are significant in their understanding of feedback;

- there are examples of when learner experiences directly inform how feedback is understood as a teacher and how teacher experiences inform understanding as a learner;

- experiences of feedback as a learner are particularly significant, and it appears student teachers begin their teacher education programmes with sometimes quite fixed ideas around feedback; their experiences as a learner within ITE can potentially reinforce these ideas;

- there are implications for ITE: the need for low-stake exploration of feedback conceptions, the value of learner experiences and reflection and critical debate around the Standards or other powerful policies;

- furthermore, there are implications for both higher education and school education; ITE providers should also take note of these as they could further inform programme design, content and approach if feedback understanding is to align.

REFLECTIONS ON **CRITICAL ISSUES**

This chapter has summarised the main findings of the book and restated how complex feedback is in itself but also re-emphasised the further complexity of feedback conceptions and experiences for student teachers in ITE. In doing so, a new conceptual model has been proposed, which recognises that understandings of feedback can have relational, moral and pedagogical themes that support or conflict with one another. The development of these understandings is fluid and open to change as the student teachers experience feedback as a learner within HE and as a practising teacher within the school setting. These overlapping contexts with their associated roles, policies, philosophies and practices mean that student teachers are continually exposed to new experiences of feedback. Given this complex and nuanced model of feedback, there are several implications and recommendations not only for ITE but also for HE and schools. This chapter has deliberately avoided presenting these implications and recommendations as 'top tips' or specific strategies, given earlier discussions about the use of formulaic technical feedback techniques. Instead, it has sought to encourage a more critical and reflective approach to feedback within and across educational contexts, exploiting any opportunities for student teachers to understand feedback from different perspectives and experiences and engage fully with the feedback debate. In relation to feedback, ITE is unique and its uniqueness needs to be fully exploited. As Hamodi et al (2017) state (in reference to formative assessment including feedback), *'It is essential to establish the link between the faculties, where future teachers are educated and actual schools where these teachers will eventually educate our children, and to deepen our scientific knowledge of the issues'* (p 187).

REFERENCES

Adcroft, A (2011) The Mythology of Feedback. *Higher Education Research & Development*, 30(4): 405–419. doi: 10.1080/07294360.2010.526096.

Ajjawi, R and Boud, D (2018) Examining the Nature and Effects of Feedback Dialogue. *Assessment & Evaluation in Higher Education*, 1–14. doi: 10.1080/02602938.2018.1434128.

Alderton, J (2019) Producing Assessment Truths: A Foucauldian Analysis of Teachers' Reorganisation of Levels in English Primary Schools. *British Journal of Sociology of Education*, 1–19. doi: 10.1080/01425692.2018.1561245.

Ali, N, Ahmed, L and Rose, S (2017) Identifying Predictors of Students' Perception of and Engagement with Assessment Feedback. *Active Learning in Higher Education*, 1469787417735609.

Allen, J, Singh, P and Rowan, L (2019) Professional Experience in Initial Teacher Education: Keeping Abreast of Change in the 21st Century. *Asia Pacific Journal of Teacher Education*, 47(4): 323–326.

Altun, S and Erden, M (2013) Self-Regulation Based Learning Strategies and Self-Efficacy Perceptions as Predictors of Male and Female Students' Mathematics Achievement. *Procedia: Social and Behavioral Sciences*, 106: 2354–2364.

Andrews, J, Robinson, D and Hutchinson, J (2017) *Closing the Gap?: Trends in Educational Attainment and Disadvantage*. August 2017.

Arthur, J, Kristjánsson, K, Cooke, S, Brown, E and Carr, D (2015) *The Good Teacher: Understanding Virtues in Practice*. Birmingham: Jubilee Centre for Character and Virtues.

Arts, J G, Jaspers, M and Joosten-ten Brinke, D (2016) A Case Study on Written Comments as a Form of Feedback in Teacher Education: So Much to Gain. *European Journal of Teacher Education*, 39(2): 159–173. doi: 10.1080/02619768.2015.1116513.

Askew, S and Lodge, C (eds) (2000) *Gifts, Ping-Pong and Loops-Linking Feedback and Learning*. London: Routledge Falmer.

Bailey, R and Garner, M (2010) Is the Feedback in Higher Education Assessment Worth the Paper it is Written On? Teachers' Reflections on Their Practices. *Teaching in Higher Education*, 15(2): 187–198. doi: 10.1080/13562511003620019.

Ball, S J (2003) The Teacher's Soul and the Terrors of Performativity. *Journal of Education Policy*, 18(2): 215–228.

Bandura, A (1991) Social Cognitive Theory of Self-Regulation. *Organizational Behavior and Human Decision Processes*, 50(2): 248–287.

Beaumont, C, O'Doherty, M and Shannon, L (2011) Reconceptualising Assessment Feedback: A Key to Improving Student Learning? *Studies in Higher Education*, 36(6): 671–687.

Beck, L G (1992) Meeting the Challenge of the Future: The Place of a Caring Ethic in Educational Administration. *American Journal of Education*, 100(4): 454–496.

Benè, K L and Bergus, G (2014) When Learners Become Teachers. *Family Medicines*, 46: 783–787.

Benn, M (2018) *Life Lessons: The Case for a National Education Service*. London: Verso.

Bernstein, B (2004) *The Structuring of Pedagogic Discourse*. London: Routledge.

Black, P and Wiliam, D (2014) *Inside the Black Box*. London: Kings College.

Black, P and Wiliam, D (1998) *Inside the Black Box: Raising Standards through Classroom Assessment*. London: Granada Learning.

Bohm, D (2013) *On Dialogue*. London: Routledge.

Boud, D and Molloy, E (2012) *Feedback in Higher and Professional Education: Understanding it and Doing it Well*. London, New York: Routledge.

Boud, D and Molloy, E (2013) Rethinking Models of Feedback for Learning: The Challenge of Design. *Assessment & Evaluation in Higher Education*, 38(6): 698–712. doi: 10.1080/02602938.2012.691462.

Boyle, W F and Charles, M (2010) Leading Learning through Assessment for Learning? *School Leadership & Management*, 30(3): 285–300. doi: 10.1080/13632434.2010.485184.

Broadfoot, P (2007) *An Introduction to Assessment*. Trowbridge: Continuum Intl Pub Group.

Broadfoot, P (1999) Empowerment or Performativity? English Assessment Policy in the Late Twentieth Century. Paper presented to the *British Education Research Association Conference*.

Brody, D L and Hadar, L L (2015) Personal Professional Trajectories of Novice and Experienced Teacher Educators in a Professional Development Community. *Teacher Development*, 19(2): 246–266. doi: 10.1080/13664530.2015.1016242.

Brooks, C (2018) What Makes Students Satisfied? A Discussion and Analysis of the UK's National Student Survey AU - Bell, Adrian R. *Journal of Further and Higher Education*, 42(8): 1118–1142. doi: 10.1080/0309877X.2017.1349886.

Brown, G T, Harris, L R and Harnett, J (2012) Teacher Beliefs about Feedback within an Assessment for Learning Environment: Endorsement of Improved Learning over Student Well-Being. *Teaching and Teacher Education*, 28(7): 968–978.

Brown, G T L (2011) Teachers' Conceptions of Assessment: Comparing Primary and Secondary Teachers in New Zealand. *Assessment Matters*, 3: 45.

Brummer, L and Kostons, D (2018) The Anonymous Reviewer: The Relationship between Perceived Expertise and the Perceptions of Peer Feedback in Higher Education AU - Dijks, Monique A. *Assessment & Evaluation in Higher Education*, 43(8): 1258–1271.

Buber, M (2013) *I and Thou*. London: Bloomsbury.

Buchanan, R (2015) Teacher Identity and Agency in an Era of Accountability. *Teachers and Teaching*, 21(6): 700–719.

Burnett, P C and Mandel, V (2010) Praise and Feedback in the Primary Classroom: Teachers' and Students' Perspectives. *Australian Journal of Educational & Developmental Psychology*, 10: 145–154.

Butler, D L and Winne, P H (1995) Feedback and Self-Regulated Learning: A Theoretical Synthesis. *Review of Educational Research*, 65(3): 245–281.

Cajkler, W and Wood, P (2016) Adapting 'Lesson Study' to Investigate Classroom Pedagogy in Initial Teacher Education: What Student-Teachers Think. *Cambridge Journal of Education*, 46(1): 1–18.

Carless, D (2015) *Excellence in University Assessment: Learning from Award-Winning Practice*. Abingdon: Routledge.

Carless, D (2018) *Student Feedback Literacy*. Available at: https://davidcarless.edu.hku.hk/student-feedback -literacy/ (accessed 30 November 2020).

Carless, D (2012) Trust and Its Role in Facilitating Dialogic Feedback, in Boud, D and Molloy, E (eds) *Feedback in Higher and Professional Education*. London: Routledge, pp 100–113.

Carless, D (2009) Trust, Distrust and Their Impact on Assessment Reform. *Assessment & Evaluation in Higher Education*, 34(1): 79–89.

Carless, D and Boud, D (2018) The Development of Student Feedback Literacy: Enabling Uptake of Feedback. *Assessment & Evaluation in Higher Education*, 43(8): 1315–1325. doi: 10.1080/02602938.2018.1463354.

Carless, D, Salter, D, Yang, M and Lam, J (2011) Developing Sustainable Feedback Practices. *Studies in Higher Education*, 36(4): 395–407.

Carter, A (2015) *Carter Review of Initial Teacher Training (ITT)*. London: Crown.

Cheng, M M, Cheng, A Y and Tang, S Y (2010) Closing the Gap between the Theory and Practice of Teaching: Implications for Teacher Education Programmes in Hong Kong. *Journal of Education for Teaching*, 36(1): 91–104.

Cheng, M M, Tang, S Y and Cheng, A Y (2014) Differences in Pedagogical Understanding among Student–Teachers in a Four-Year Initial Teacher Education Programme. *Teachers and Teaching*, 20(2): 152–169.

Christie, F (1995) Pedagogic Discourse in the Primary School. *Linguistics and Education*, 7(3): 221–242.

Clarke, M and Phelan, A M (2017) *Teacher Education and the Political: The Power of Negative Thinking*. London: Routledge, Taylor & Francis Group.

Clarke, S (2003) *Enriching Feedback in the Primary Classroom: Oral and Written Feedback from Teachers and Children*. London: Hodder and Stoughton.

Clarke, S (2014) *Outstanding Formative Assessment: Culture and Practice*. Oxon: Hachette UK.

Clouder, L and Adefila, A (2016) The 'Gift Exchange': A Metaphor for Understanding the Relationship between Educator Commitment and Student Effort on. *International Journal of Practice-Based Learning in Health and Social Care*, 2(2): 54–64.

Cochran-Smith, M (2003) The Unforgiving Complexity of Teaching: Avoiding Simplicity in the Age of Accountability. *Journal of Teacher Education*, 54(1): 3–5.

Cousin, G (2006) An Introduction to Threshold Concepts. *Planet*, 17(1): 4–5. doi: 10.11120/plan.2006.00170004.

Crisp, B R (2007) Is it Worth the Effort? How Feedback Influences Students' Subsequent Submission of Assessable Work. *Assessment & Evaluation in Higher Education*, 32(5): 571–581.

Dargusch, J and Charteris, J (2018) Nobody Is Watching but Everything I Do Is Measured: Teacher Accountability, Learner Agency and the Crisis of Control. *Australian Journal of Teacher Education*, 43(10): 24–40.

Darling-Hammond, L (2017) Teacher Education Around the World: What Can We Learn from International Practice? *European Journal of Teacher Education*, 40(3): 291–309.

Daugherty, R (2004) National Curriculum Assessment: a review of policy 1987–1994. London: Routledge.

Dawson, P, Henderson, M, Mahoney, P, Phillips, M, Ryan, T, Boud, D, et al. (2018) What Makes for Effective Feedback: Staff and Student Perspectives. *Assessment & Evaluation in Higher Education*, 1–12.

Day, C (2002) School Reform and Transitions in Teacher Professionalism and Identity. *International Journal of Educational Research*, 37(8): 677–692.

Deci, E L and Ryan, R M (2008) Self-Determination Theory: A Macrotheory of Human Motivation, Development, and Health. *Canadian Psychology/Psychologie Canadienne*, 49(3): 182.

Defeyter, M A and McPartlin, P L (2007) Helping Students Understand Essay Marking Criteria and Feedback. *Psychology Teaching Review*, 13(1): 23–33.

DeLuca, C, Luu, K, Sun, Y and Klinger, D A (2012) Assessment for Learning in the Classroom: Barriers to Implementation and Possibilities for Teacher Professional Learning. *Assessment Matters*, 4, p 5.

Department for Education (2019a) *Early Career Framework*. London: Crown.

Department for Education (2016) *Eliminating Unnecessary Workload around Marking*. London: Department for Education.

Department for Education (2021) *Initial Teacher Training (ITT) Market Review: Overview*. Available at: https://www.gov.uk/government/publications/initial-teacher-training-itt-market-review/initial-teacher-training-itt-market-review-overview (accessed 8 January 2021).

Department for Education (2019b) *ITT Core Content Framework*. London: Crown.

Department of Education and Science (1980) *A View of the Curriculum HMI Series: Matters for Discussion No 11*. London: Her Majesty's Stationery Office.

DfE (2012) *Teachers' Standards: Guidance for School Leaders, School Staff and Governing Bodies.* The Stationery Office: Crown.

Dixon, H R, Hawe, E and Parr, J (2011) Enacting Assessment for Learning: the Beliefs Practice Nexus. *Assessment in Education: Principles, Policy & Practice*, 18(4): 365–379.

Donche, V and Van Petegem, P (2009) The Development of Learning Patterns of Student Teachers: A Cross-Sectional and Longitudinal Study. *Higher Education*, 57(4): 463–475.

Edwards, A (1998) Mentoring Student Teachers in Primary Schools: Assisting Student Teachers to Become Learners. *European Journal of Teacher Education*, 21(1): 47–62.

Ell, F, Haigh, M, Cochran-Smith, M, Grudnoff, L, Ludlow, L and Hill, M (2017) Mapping a Complex System: What Influences Teacher Learning during Initial Teacher Education? *Asia Pacific Journal of Teacher Education*, 45(4): 327–345.

Endedijk, M D, Vermunt, J D, Meijer, P C and Brekelmans, M (2014) Students' Development in Self-Regulated Learning in Postgraduate Professional Education: A Longitudinal Study. *Studies in Higher Education*, 39(7): 1116–1138.

Espasa, A and Martinez-Melo, M (2019) The Art of Questioning in Online Learning Environments: The Potentialities of Feedback in Writing AU - Guasch, Teresa. *Assessment & Evaluation in Higher Education*, 44(1): 111–123. doi: 10.1080/02602938.2018.1479373.

Esterhazy, R (2018) What Matters for Productive Feedback? Disciplinary Practices and Their Relational Dynamics. *Assessment & Evaluation in Higher Education*, 43(8): 1302–1314. doi: 10.1080/02602938.2018.1463353.

Eva, K W, Armson, H, Holmboe, E, Lockyer, J, Loney, E, Mann, K and Sargeant, J (2012) Factors Influencing Responsiveness to Feedback: On the Interplay Between Fear, Confidence, and Reasoning Processes. *Advances in Health Sciences Education*, 17(1): 15–26.

Evans, C (2016) *Enhancing Assessment Feedback Practice in Higher Education: The EAT Framework.* Southampton: University of Southampton.

Evans, C (2013) Making Sense of Assessment Feedback in Higher Education. *Review of Educational Research*, 83(1): 70–120.

Fairclough, N (1992) *Discourse and Social Change.* Cambridge: Polity Press.

Flores, M (2020) Learning to Teach: Knowledge, Competences and Support in Initial Teacher Education and in the Early Years of Teaching. *European Journal of Teacher Education*, 43(2): 127–130.

Flores, M (2018) Linking Teaching and Research in Initial Teacher Education: Knowledge Mobilisation and Research-Informed Practice. *Journal of Education for Teaching*, 44(5): 621–636.

Foucault, M (2001) *Fearless Speech.* Los Angeles: Semiotext.

Friedman, I A (2016) Being a Teacher: Altruistic and Narcissistic Expectations of Pre-service Teachers. *Teachers and Teaching*, 22(5): 625–648. doi: 10.1080/13540602.2016.1158469.

Friesen, M D and Besley, S C (2013) Teacher Identity Development in the First Year of Teacher Education: A Developmental and Social Psychological Perspective. *Teaching and Teacher Education*, 36: 23–32.

Furlong, J and Maynard, T (1995) *Mentoring Student Teachers: The Growth of Professional Knowledge.* London: Psychology Press.

Gamlem, S M and Munthe, E (2014) Mapping the Quality of Feedback to Support Students' Learning in Lower Secondary Classrooms. *Cambridge Journal of Education*, 44(1): 75–92. doi: 10.1080/0305764X.2013.855171.

Gaskill, P J and Woolfolk Hoy, A (2002) Self-Efficacy and Self-Regulated Learning: The Dynamic Duo in School Performance, in Aronson, J (ed) *Improving Academic Achievement.* San Diego: Academic Press, pp 185–208.

George, R and Maguire, M (2019) Choice and Diversity in English Initial Teacher Education (ITE): Trainees' Perspectives. *European Journal of Teacher Education*, 42(1): 19–35.

Gibbs, G and Simpson, C (2004) Conditions under Which Assessment Supports Students' Learning. *Learning and Teaching in Higher Education*, 1(1): 3–31.

Glover, C and Brown, E (2006) Written Feedback for Students: Too Much, Too Detailed or Too Incomprehensible to Be Effective? *Bioscience Education*, 1(7): 1–16.

Gosselin, K P, Northcote, M, Reynaud, D, et al. (2016) Development of an Evidence-Based Professional Learning Program Informed by Online Teachers' Self-Efficacy and Threshold Concepts. *Online Learning*, 20(3). doi: 10.24059/olj.v20i3.648.

Grossman, P L, Valencia, S W, Evans, K, Thompson, C, Martin, S and Place, N (2000) Transitions into Teaching: Learning to Teach Writing in Teacher Education and Beyond. *Journal of Literacy Research*, 32(4): 631–662.

Guilherme, A. and Morgan, W J (2009) Martin Buber's Philosophy of Education and Its Implications for Adult Non-Formal Education. *International Journal of Lifelong Education*, 28(5): 565–581. doi: 10.1080/02601370903189989.

Gul, R B, Tharani, A, Lakhani, A, Rizvi, N F and Ali, S K (2016) Teachers' Perceptions and Practices of Written Feedback in Higher Education. *World Journal of Education*, 6(3): 10.

Hamodi, C, López-Pastor, V M and López-Pastor, A T (2017) If I Experience Formative Assessment Whilst Studying at University, Will I Put it into Practice Later as a Teacher? Formative and Shared Assessment in Initial Teacher Education (ITE). *European Journal of Teacher Education*, 40(2), pp171–190.

Hargreaves, E (2005) Assessment for Learning? Thinking Outside the (Black) Box. *Cambridge Journal of Education*, 35(2): 213–224. doi: 10.1080/03057640500146880.

Hargreaves, E (2013) Inquiring into Children's Experiences of Teacher Feedback: Reconceptualising Assessment for Learning. *Oxford Review of Education*, 39(2): 229–246.

Harlen, W (2004) Rethinking the Teacher's Role in Assessment. Paper presented at the *British Research Assessment Annual Conference*, University of Manchester, (pp 16–18). September 2004. Retrieved from http://www.leeds.ac.uk/educol/documents/00003775.htm.

Hattie, J (2003) *Teachers Make a Difference, What is the Research Evidence?* Melbourne. October 2003. Australian Council for Educational Research.

Hattie, J (2009) *Visible Learning: A Synthesis of Over 800 Meta-Analyses Relating to Achievement*. Abingdon: Routledge.

Hattie, J and Clarke, S (2018) *Visible Learning: Feedback*. Abingdon: Routledge.

Hattie, J and Timperley, H (2007) The Power of Feedback. *Review of Educational Research*, 77(1): 81–112.

Heinz, M (2015) Why Choose Teaching? An International Review of Empirical Studies Exploring Student Teachers' Career Motivations and Levels of Commitment to Teaching. *Educational Research and Evaluation*, 21(3): 258–297. doi: 10.1080/13803611.2015.1018278.

Higgins, R, Hartley, P and Skelton, A (2001) Getting the Message Across: The Problem of Communicating Assessment Feedback. *Teaching in Higher Education*, 6(2): 269–274.

Ipsos, M O R I (2021) *National Student Survey*. Available at: https://www.thestudentsurvey.com/ (accessed 19 January 2020).

Jarvis, P (1995) Teachers and Learners in Adult Education: Transaction or Moral Interaction? *Studies in the Education of Adults*, 27(1): 24–35. doi: 10.1080/02660830.1995.11730613.

Johnson, C E, Keating, J L, Boud, D J, Dalton, M, Kiegaldie, D, Hay, M, et al. (2016) Identifying Educator Behaviours for High Quality Verbal Feedback in Health Professions Education: Literature Review and Expert Refinement. *BMC Medical Education*, 16(1): 96.

Kahu, E R (2008) Feedback: The Heart of Good Pedagogy. *New Zealand Annual Review of Education*, 17: 187–197.

Kirton, A, Hallam, S, Peffers, J, Robertson, P and Stobart, G (2007) Revolution, Evolution or a Trojan Horse? Piloting Assessment for Learning in Some Scottish Primary Schools. *British Educational Research Journal*, 33(4): 605–627.

Korthagen, F A J (2010) How Teacher Education can Make a Difference. *Journal of Education for Teaching*, 36(4): 407–423.

Korthagen, F A J (2004) In Search of the Essence of a Good Teacher: Towards a More Holistic Approach in Teacher Education. *Teaching and Teacher Education*, 20(1): 77–97. doi: 10.1016/j.tate.2003.10.002.

Kwan, T and Lopez-Real, F (2005) Mentors' Perceptions of Their Roles in Mentoring Student Teachers. *Asia-Pacific Journal of Teacher Education*, 33(3): 275–287.

Laws, D (2013) *Closing the Achievement Gap*. Available at: https://www.gov.uk/government/speeches/closin g-the-achievement-gap (accessed 3 December 2020).

Leach, T (2019) Satisfied with What? Contested Assumptions about Student Expectations and Satisfaction in Higher Education. *Research in Post-Compulsory Education*, 24(2–3): 155–172. doi: 10.1080/13596748.2019.1596410.

Leckie, G and Goldstein, H (2017) The Evolution of School League Tables in England 1992–2016: 'Contextual Value-Added', 'Expected Progress' and 'Progress 8'. *British Educational Research Journal*, 43(2): 193–212.

Lee, S and Schallert, D L (2016) Becoming a Teacher: Coordinating Past, Present, and Future Selves with Perspectival Understandings about Teaching. *Teaching and Teacher Education*, 56: 72–83.

Löfström, E and Poom-Valickis, K (2013) Beliefs about Teaching: Persistent or Malleable? A Longitudinal Study of Prospective Student Teachers' Beliefs. *Teaching and Teacher Education*, 35: 104–113. doi: 10.1016/j.tate.2013.06.004.

Lofthouse, R M (2018) Re-imagining Mentoring as a Dynamic Hub in the Transformation of Initial Teacher Education. *International Journal of Mentoring and Coaching in Education*, 7(3): 248–260.

Lortie, D C (1975) *Schoolteacher: A Sociological Study*. Chicago: University of Chicago Press.

Mao, S S and Crosthwaite, P (2019) Investigating Written Corrective Feedback:(Mis) Alignment of Teachers' Beliefs and Practice. *Journal of Second Language Writing*, 45: 46–60.

Maxwell, B and Schwimmer, M (2016) Seeking the Elusive Ethical Base of Teacher Professionalism in Canadian Codes of Ethics. *Teaching and Teacher Education*, 59: 468–480.

McArthur, J (2018) *Assessment for Social Justice: Perspectives and Practices within Higher Education*. London: Bloomsbury Academic Publishing.

Meyer, J H F and Land, R (2005) Threshold Concepts and Troublesome Knowledge (2): Epistemological Considerations and a Conceptual Framework for Teaching and Learning. *Higher Education*, 49(3): 373–388. DOI: 10.1007/s10734-004-6779-5.

Molloy, E, Borrell-Carrió, F and Epstein, R (2012) The Impact of Emotions in Feedback, in Boud, D and Molloy, E (eds) *Feedback in Higher and Professional Education* Abingdon: Routledge, pp 60–81.

Molloy, E and Boud, D (2013) Changing Conceptions of Feedback. *Feedback in Higher and Professional Education: Understanding it and Doing it Well*, pp 11–23. Routledge.

Murtagh, L (2014) The Motivational Paradox of Feedback: Teacher and Student Perceptions. *The Curriculum Journal*, 25(4): 516–541. doi: 10.1080/09585176.2014.944197.

Mutch, A (2003) Exploring the Practice of Feedback to Students. *Active Learning in Higher Education*, 4(1): 24–38.

Mutton, T, Burn, K and Menter, I (2017) Deconstructing the Carter Review: Competing Conceptions of Quality in England's 'School-Led' System of Initial Teacher Education. *Journal of Education Policy*, 32(1): 14–33.

Naismith, L M and Lajoie, S P (2018) Motivation and Emotion Predict Medical Students' Attention to Computer-Based Feedback. *Advances in Health Sciences Education*, 1–21.

Neve, H, Wearn, A and Collett, T (2016) What are Threshold Concepts and How Can They Inform Medical Education? *Medical Teacher*, 38(8): 850–853. doi: 10.3109/0142159X.2015.1112889.

Ní Chróinín, D and O'Sullivan, M (2014) From Initial Teacher Education through Induction and Beyond: A Longitudinal Study of Primary Teacher Beliefs. *Irish Educational Studies*, 33(4): 451–466. doi: 10.1080/03323315.2014.984387.

Nicol, D (2010) From Monologue to Dialogue: Improving Written Feedback Processes in Mass Higher Education. *Assessment & Evaluation in Higher Education*, 35(5): 501–517.

Nicol, D and Macfarlane-Dick, D (2006) Formative Assessment and Self-Regulated Learning: A Model and Seven Principles of Good Feedback Practice. *Studies in Higher Education*, 31(2): 199–218. doi: 10.1080/03075070600572090.

Nicol, D and Macfarlane-Dick, D (2004) *Rethinking Formative Assessment in HE: A Theoretical Model and Seven Principles of Good Feedback Practice*. Higher Education Academy.

Nicola-Richmond, K, Pépin, G, Larkin, H, et al. (2018) Threshold Concepts in Higher Education: A Synthesis of the Literature Relating to Measurement of Threshold Crossing. *Higher Education Research & Development*, 37(1): 101–114. DOI: 10.1080/07294360.2017.1339181.

Nilsson, P (2008) *Learning to Teach and Teaching to Learn*. PhD, Norrköping: Department of Social and Welfare Studies, Linköping University.

Ofsted (2020) *Initial Teacher Education Inspection Framework and Handbook*. Manchester: Crown.

Ofsted (2019) *Education Inspection Framework (EIF)*. Available at: https://www.gov.uk/government/publications/education-inspection-framework (accessed 8 January 2021).

Ofsted (2018) *Ofsted Inspections: Myths*. Available at: https://www.gov.uk/government/publications/school-inspection-handbook-from-september-2015/ofsted-inspections-mythbusting#pupils-work (accessed 26 January 2019).

Orrell, J (2006) Feedback on Learning Achievement: Rhetoric and Reality. *Teaching in Higher Education*, 11(4): 441–456.

Oser, F K (2014) Professional Morality: A Discourse Approach (the Case of the Teaching Profession), in Heinrichs, K, Oser, F and Lovat, T (eds) *Handbook of Moral Behavior and Development*. Hillsdale, NJ: Psychology Press, pp 213–250.

Pantić, N and Florian, L (2015) Developing Teachers as Agents of Inclusion and Social Justice. *Education Inquiry*, 6(3): 27311.

Paterson, C, Paterson, N, Jackson, W and Work, F (2020) What Are Students' Needs and Preferences for Academic Feedback in Higher Education? A Systematic Review. *Nurse Education Today*, 85: 104236.

Perkins, D (1999) The Many Faces of Constructivism. *Educational Leadership*, 57(3): 6–11.

Peterson, E R and Irving, S E (2008) Secondary School Students' Conceptions of Assessment and Feedback. *Learning and Instruction*, 18(3): 238–250.

Pitt, E and Winstone, N (2018) The Impact of Anonymous Marking on Students' Perceptions of Fairness, Feedback and Relationships with Lecturers. *Assessment & Evaluation in Higher Education*, 1–11. doi: 10.1080/02602938.2018.1437594.

Poskitt, J (2014) Transforming Professional Learning and Practice in Assessment for Learning. *The Curriculum Journal*, 25(4): 542–566.

Ramaprasad, A (1983) On the Definition of Feedback. *Behavioral Science*, 28(1): 4–13.

Rea, S, Hill, R and Dunford, J (2013) *Closing the gap: how system leaders and schools can work together*. London: National College for Teaching and Leadership/Department for Education.

Reinholz, D (2016) The Assessment Cycle: A Model for Learning Through Peer Assessment. *Assessment & Evaluation in Higher Education*, 41(2): 301–315.

Richards, G and Richardson, R (2019) *Reducing Teachers' Marking Workload and Developing Pupils' Learning: How to Create More Impact with Less Marking*. Abingdon: Routledge.

Richardson, P W and Watt, H M (2006) Who Chooses Teaching and Why? Profiling Characteristics and Motivations Across Three Australian Universities. *Asia-Pacific Journal of Teacher Education*, 34(1): 27–56. doi: 10.1080/13598660500480290.

Robinson, A (2011) *In theory Bakhtin: Dialogism, Polyphony and Heteroglossia*. Available at: https://ceasefi remagazine.co.uk/in-theory-bakhtin-1/ (accessed 20 March 2019).

Rodgers, C R and Scott, K H (2008) The Development of the Personal Self and Professional Identity in Learning to Teach, in Cochran-Smith, M, Feiman-Nemser, S, Demers, K and McIntyre, J (eds) *Handbook of Research on Teacher Education: Enduring Questions and Changing Contexts*. New York: Routledge/Taylor & Francis Group, pp 432–755.

Sadler, D R (2010) Beyond Feedback: Developing Student Capability in Complex Appraisal. *Assessment & Evaluation in Higher Education*, 35(5): 535–550.

Sadler, D R (1989) Formative Assessment and the Design of Instructional Systems. *Instructional Science*, 18(2): 119–144.

Salifu, I and Agbenyega, J S (2016) Teacher Motivation and Identity Formation: Issues Affecting Professional Practice. *MIER Journal of Educational Studies, Trends and Practices*, 3(1).

Sambell, K (2016) Assessment and Feedback in Higher Education: Considerable Room for Improvement? *Student Engagement in Higher Education*, 1(1).

Sambell, K, Gibson, M and Montgomery, C (2007) *Rethinking Feedback: An Assessment for Learning Perspective*. Bristol: ESCalate.

Sambell, K and McDowell, L (1998) The Construction of the Hidden Curriculum: Messages and Meanings in the Assessment of Student Learning. *Assessment & Evaluation in Higher Education*, 23(4): 391–402. doi: 10.1080/0260293980230406.

Savvidou, C (2018) Exploring the Pedagogy of Online Feedback in Supporting Distance Learners, in Llevot-Calvet, N and Bernad-Cavero, O (eds) *Advanced Learning and Teaching Environments-Innovation, Contents and Methods*. London: IntechOpen, pp 103–121.

Sayer, A (2000) Moral Economy and Political Economy. *Studies in Political Economy*, 61(1): 79–103.

Schmulian, A and Coetzee, S A (2019) Students' Experience of Team Assessment with Immediate Feedback in a Large Accounting Class. *Assessment & Evaluation in Higher Education*, 44(4): 516–532. doi: 10.1080/02602938.2018.1522295.

Schüler, J, Sheldon, K M and Fröhlich, S M (2010) Implicit Need for Achievement Moderates the Relationship between Competence Need Satisfaction and Subsequent Motivation. *Journal of Research in Personality*, 44(1): 1–12.

Scriven, M (1967) The Methodology of Evaluation In Tyler, RW, Gagne, RM, Scriven, M (ed): Perspectives of Curriculum Evaluation: Book The Methodology of Evaluation, in Tyler, Rw, Gagne, Rm, Scriven, M. (eds) *Perspectives of Curriculum Evaluation*. Chicago: Rand McNally.

Sealy, C (2018) *How We Stopped Marking*. Available at: https://teaching.blog.gov.uk/2018/07/23/how-we-sto pped-marking/ (accessed 8 January 2021).

Sharples, J, Slavin, R, Chambers, B and Sharp, C (2011) *Effective Classroom Strategies for Closing the Gap in Educational Achievement for Children and Young People Living in Poverty, Including White Working-Class Boys*. London: C4EO.

Sluijsmans, D M, Brand-Gruwel, S and van Merriënboer, J J (2002) Peer Assessment Training in Teacher Education: Effects on Performance and Perceptions. *Assessment & Evaluation in Higher Education*, 27(5): 443–454.

Spielman, A (2018) *HMCI's Commentary: Recent Primary and Secondary Curriculum Research*. Available at: https://www.gov.uk/government/speeches/hmci-commentary-curriculum-and-the-new-education-inspection-framework (accessed 8 January 2021).

Stern, J (2007) Mattering: What it Means to Matter in School. *Education*, 35(3): 283–293.

Strijbos, J and Ufer, S (2019) Preservice Mathematics Teachers' Beliefs about Peer Feedback, Perceptions of Their Peer Feedback Message, and Emotions as Predictors of Peer Feedback Accuracy and Comprehension of the Learning Task AU - Alqassab, Maryam. *Assessment & Evaluation in Higher Education*, 44(1): 139–154. doi: 10.1080/02602938.2018.1485012.

Taubman, P (2012) *Disavowed Knowledge: Psychoanalysis, Education, and Teaching*. London: Routledge.

The Sutton Trust (2020) EEP Teacher Toolkit. Available at: https://educationendowmentfoundation.org.uk/evidence-summaries/teaching-learning-toolkit/ (accessed 12 December 2020).

Thoutenhoofd, E D and Pirrie, A (2015) From Self-Regulation to Learning to Learn: Observations on the Construction of Self and Learning. *British Educational Research Journal*, 41(1): 72–84.

Timmerman, B C, Feldon, D, Maher, M, et al. (2013) Performance-Based Assessment of Graduate Student Research Skills: Timing, Trajectory, and Potential Thresholds. *Studies in Higher Education*, 38(5): 693–710. doi: 10.1080/03075079.2011.590971.

Universities' Council for the Education of Teachers (2020) UCET Statement on the Core Content Framework and OfSTED Inspection Framework. Available at: https://www.ucet.ac.uk/11973/ucet-statement-on-the-core-content-framework-and-ofsted-inspection-framework-23rd-june-2020 (accessed 8 January 2021).

Universities' Council for the Education of Teachers (2021) UCET Statement on the DfE Review of the ITE Market and the Institute for Teaching. Available at: https://www.ucet.ac.uk/12507/ucet-statement-on-the-dfe-review-of-the-ite-market-and-the-institute-for-teaching (accessed 8 January 2021).

van den Bergh, L, Ros, A and Beijaard, D (2013) Teacher Feedback during Active Learning: Current Practices in Primary Schools. *British Journal of Educational Psychology*, 83(2): 341–362.

Van Geert, P and Steenbeek, H (2014) The Good, the Bad and the Ugly? The Dynamic Interplay between Educational Practice, Policy and Research. *Complicity: An International Journal of Complexity and Education*, 11(2).

Walker, C, Gleaves, A and Grey, J (2006) Can Students within Higher Education Learn to Be Resilient and, Educationally Speaking, Does it Matter? *Educational Studies*, 32(3): 251–264. doi: 10.1080/03055690600631184.

Ward, H (2008) Assessment for Learning has Fallen Prey to Gimmicks. *Times Educational Supplement*, 17 October. Available at: https://www.tes.com/news/assessment-learning-has-fallen-prey-gimmicks-says-critic (accessed 8 January 2021).

Watt, H M, Richardson, P W, Klusmann, U, Kunter, M, Beyer, B, Trautwein, U and Baumert, J (2012) Motivations for Choosing Teaching as a Career: An International Comparison Using the FIT-Choice Scale. *Teaching and Teacher Education*, 28(6): 791–805.

Wiliam, D (2011) *Embedded Formative Assessment*. Bloomington: Solution Tree Press.

Williamson, B (2017) *Big Data in Education: The Digital Future of Learning, Policy and Practice*. London: SAGE.

Wilson, J (2014) *Closing the Gap with the New Primary National Curriculum* London: National College for Teaching and Leadership.

Winstone, N (2018) *How Are Cultures of Feedback Practice Shaped by Accountability and Quality Assurance Agendas?* SRHE.

Winstone, N and Carless, D (2019) *Designing Effective Feedback Processes in Higher Education: A Learning-Focused Approach.* London: Routledge.

Winter, P D and Linehan, M J (2014) Bernstein's Theory of Pedagogic Discourse as a Theoretical Framework for Educators Studying Student Radiographers' Interpretation of Normality vs. Abnormality. *Radiography*, 20(1): 58–64.

Wisniewski, B, Zierer, K and Hattie, J (2020) The Power of Feedback Revisited: A Meta-Analysis of Educational Feedback Research. *Frontiers in Psychology*, 10: 3087. doi: 10.3389/fpsyg.2019.03087.

Xu, Y and Brown, G T (2016) Teacher Assessment Literacy in Practice: A Reconceptualization. *Teaching and Teacher Education*, 58: 149–162.

Yang, M and Carless, D (2013) The Feedback Triangle and the Enhancement of Dialogic Feedback Processes. *Teaching in Higher Education*, 18(3): 285–297.

Zhang, L and Zheng, Y (2018) Feedback as an Assessment for Learning Tool: How Useful Can it Be? *Assessment & Evaluation in Higher Education*, 1–13.

Zimmerman, A (2019) Illuminating Teacher Educators' Self-Understanding through the Study of Relationships in the Teacher Education Classroom. *Fostering a Relational Pedagogy: Self-Study as Transformative Praxis*, pp 180. Leiden, the Netherlands: Brill.

Zumbrunn, S, Tadlock, J and Roberts, E D (2011) Encouraging Self-Regulated Learning in the Classroom: A Review of the Literature. *Metropolitan Educational Research Consortium (MERC)*, pp 1–28.

INDEX

Printed in Poland
by Amazon Fulfillment
Poland Sp. z o.o., Wrocław

81587956R00054